It's another Quality Book from CGP

This book is for anyone studying OCR GCSE Graphics.

Let's face it, D&T is pretty hard-going — you've got a whole load of technical stuff to learn on top of doing your project.

Happily this CGP book helps to take the headache out of all that learning. We've explained all the technical stuff — and drawn plenty of pictures to make the whole thing that bit clearer. Plus we've stuck in some handy hints to help make your project a winner, and some tips on exam technique.

And in true CGP style it's got some daft bits in to try and make the whole experience at least vaguely entertaining for you.

What CGP is all about

Our sole aim here at CGP is to produce the highest quality books — carefully written, immaculately presented and dangerously close to being funny.

Then we work our socks off to get them out to you — at the cheapest possible prices.

Contents

Section Four — Types of Drawings

Section Five — Social and Environmental Issues

Section Six — Manufacturing Systems

Published by Coordination Group Publications Ltd.

Editors:
Katie Braid, Polly Cotterill, Katherine Craig, Ben Fletcher, Rosie Gillham, Sarah Hilton,
Adam Moorhouse, Hayley Thompson, Luke von Kotze.

Contributors:
Ryan Ball, Juliet Gibson, Debbie McGrory, Anthony Wilcock.

With thanks to Adrian Lee for the content review.
With thanks to Paul Jordin, Simon Little, Andy Park and Lesley Tillotson for the proofreading.

With thanks to Laura Stoney for the copyright research.

ISBN: 978 1 84762 355 3

Groovy website: www.cgpbooks.co.uk
Jolly bits of clipart from CorelDRAW®

With thanks to the Forest Stewardship Council for permission to reproduce the logo on page 4,
© 1996 Forest Stewardship Council A.C.

With thanks to BSI for permission to reproduce the Kitemark symbol on page 61. Kitemark and the
Kitemark symbol are registered trademarks of BSI. For more information visit www.kitemark.com.

The motorway sign image on page 63 is reproduced under the terms of Crown Copyright Policy
Guidance issued by HMSO.

With thanks to Valpak for permission to reproduce the Green Dot® symbol on page 65.

Every effort has been made to locate copyright holders and obtain permission to reproduce sources.
For those sources where it has been difficult to trace the originator of the work, we would be grateful for
information. If any copyright holder would like us to make an amendment to the acknowledgements,
please notify us and we will gladly update the book at the next reprint. Thank you.

Printed by Elanders Hindson Ltd, Newcastle upon Tyne.

Based on the classic CGP style created by Richard Parsons.

Project Advice

Unlike most subjects, in D&T you actually get to <u>make something useful</u> (well, hopefully).

The <u>Projects</u> are Worth <u>60%</u> of Your <u>GCSE</u>

1) Your D&T <u>projects</u> are called '<u>controlled assessments</u>'.

2) There are <u>two projects</u> — the first one is about designing and making a <u>prototype</u>, and the other one is about designing and making a fully functioning quality <u>product</u>.

3) Your teacher will give you as much help as they're allowed to by the exam board, so do <u>ask them</u>... but mostly it's <u>up to you</u> to make a <u>good job</u> of your projects.

4) You can dip into this book for a bit of extra help. Section 1 is all about the design process, so if you're not sure <u>where to start</u>, that might be a good place to look.

5) If you're wondering about a particular <u>detail</u> — what type of <u>adhesive</u> to use, say — it's probably quickest to look that up in the <u>index</u> and go straight to that page.

The Exam Board <u>Sets the Themes</u>

You'll be given a range of <u>themes</u> and <u>starting points</u> to choose your projects from.
You've got to pick <u>different themes</u> for your two projects though.

> EXAMPLE
> An eye-catching book for young children.

Only Put <u>Relevant Stuff</u> in Your <u>Folder</u>

1) Your <u>teacher</u> will give you plenty of guidance on what needs to go in your folder, but you can use this section of the book for a <u>reminder</u>.

2) The next two pages tell you <u>what you can get marks for</u> and give you a few tips on <u>how</u> to get them.

3) You should include lots of <u>info</u> and <u>detail</u>... but your work needs to be <u>concise</u> and <u>to the point</u>.

4) So don't <u>waffle</u> and don't waste space on <u>irrelevant</u> stuff. For example:

> Say you've analysed some existing <u>restaurant menus</u> — don't <u>bore the examiners stupid</u> with detailed descriptions of the menus from every restaurant within a ten mile radius of your school.
> A <u>brief summary</u> of your research findings is all that's needed — then the really important thing to say is how those findings <u>helped you decide</u> on the design of <u>your product</u>.

Include Plenty of <u>Photos</u>

<u>DO</u> put in lots of <u>photos</u>. The examiners love this. They want to see photos of:

Here's me with the manufacturer's specification.

- Your <u>final product</u> (obviously) — take photos from <u>different angles</u> and show what your product looks like when it's actually <u>being used</u>.

- Any <u>models</u> you make (see p. 18). Don't just put in photos of the ones that worked. In fact, the ones that <u>didn't quite work</u> are more useful because then you can explain <u>what was wrong</u> and how you fixed it.

- The <u>intermediate stages</u> of making your final product — part of the way through the assembly process, say — to show <u>how you constructed</u> it.

Controlled Assessment — nope, it's not funny...

Most of the controlled assessment marks depend on the <u>sheer brilliance</u> of your <u>folders</u>, so don't worry if your products aren't perfect — you'll get loads of marks for being dead <u>critical</u> in your <u>evaluations</u>.

Project Advice

The first project needs to show the examiner how you've got from the <u>theme</u> to a <u>working prototype</u>. These are the things that you need to do to get top marks...

Creativity _is Worth 10 Marks_

1) Research <u>existing products</u> — look around town and in different shops to see what kind of products are already out there, and get some ideas from books or the Internet.

2) Identify and research your <u>target market</u> — find out what they need and want, and will be more likely to buy.

3) Look at the <u>trends</u> in existing products — you'll need to take this into account when thinking of ideas.

4) <u>Analyse</u> your <u>research</u> — summarise your findings and say how they'll influence your design.

Designing _is Worth 14 Marks_

1) Write a <u>design specification</u> based on your design brief and your research analysis (see pages 12-13).

2) Come up with a range of <u>creative</u> and <u>innovative ideas</u> to meet your design specification.

3) <u>Communicate</u> your design ideas using appropriate drawing techniques and ICT. <u>Annotate</u> (add notes to) your drawings so it's clear what things are and how they work, etc.

4) Choose your <u>best</u> design idea and make sure that you communicate all the <u>details</u> of it really clearly — this design should be the one that most closely matches the design specification.

5) Think about what impact your design will have on the <u>environment</u> (see pages 62-67).

Making _is Worth 28 Marks_

1) <u>Model</u> your idea (see page 18) to see if there are any <u>problems</u> with it, and make <u>modifications</u> to your design to keep improving it. Remember to take photos of the various things you try out.

2) Check your design is suitable for the needs of your <u>target market</u>.

3) Use appropriate <u>materials</u> and <u>equipment</u> — explain why they're appropriate, e.g. because they're sustainable.

4) Work <u>accurately</u> and <u>skilfully</u>, using the right techniques and tools for the job — use CAM if appropriate and carry out quality control checks at each stage of making.

5) Work <u>safely</u> and show that you know what you're doing — know the risks and how to use tools safely.

6) <u>Record</u> the key stages involved in making your product — write detailed notes as well as taking photos.

7) Don't worry if <u>problems</u> spring up along the way — you'll get marks for identifying and fixing any problems.

Evaluating _is Worth 8 Marks_

1) This is all about <u>critically evaluating</u> your prototype (picking out the good and bad points). What went well? What worked and what didn't? What would you change and why?

2) Your prototype is unlikely to be perfect, so suggest some <u>improvements</u> you could make.

3) Evaluate your <u>designing</u>, <u>modelling</u> and <u>making</u> processes — and suggest how you'd make them better.

4) Present your information in a <u>clear</u> and <u>structured</u> way — plan what you're going to write and use ICT.

5) Use <u>specialist terms</u> — but only if you know what they mean (use the glossary on pages 82-84).

6) Double check your <u>spelling</u>, <u>grammar</u> and <u>punctuation</u> to make sure you don't lose out on marks.

Tell the story of your design — and give it a happy ending...

You'd scarcely believe how much examiners <u>hate</u> wading through pages and pages of designs that people have <u>copied off the Internet</u>. So do all your research — and then develop your own <u>original ideas</u>.

Project Advice

Your second project needs to show in detail how you've <u>designed</u> and <u>made</u> a quality product. You get marks for the same kind of things as in the first project — but it's a little more about your <u>final product</u>.

Designing *is Worth* 16 Marks

1) Produce a detailed <u>design specification</u> based on the design brief and your research.
2) Come up with a range of creative <u>design ideas</u> and <u>record</u> them.
3) Use all the techniques you've learnt to do some super <u>drawings</u> with lots of <u>annotations</u>.
4) Choose your <u>best</u> idea and develop it further — clearly showing all the <u>details</u> of your design.

Making *is Worth* 36 Marks

1) <u>Plan</u> and <u>organise</u> all the different stages, e.g. by using a flow chart or a Gantt chart (see page 21).
2) <u>Model</u> your design and make any <u>improvements</u>, making sure the product meets the <u>user's needs</u>.
3) Don't ignore any <u>problems</u> — deal with them as they come up.
4) Use the most appropriate <u>materials</u>, <u>equipment</u> and <u>tools</u> available to you.
5) <u>Shape</u>, <u>assemble</u> and <u>finish</u> your product skilfully, and always work <u>safely</u>.
6) <u>Record</u> the key stages involved in the making process.
7) <u>Check</u> your product meets your product specification — tick off each point it covers.

Evaluating *is Worth* 8 Marks

1) <u>Critically evaluate</u> your finished product against your product specification
   — has it turned out how you expected? What would you change next time?
2) Do some serious <u>testing</u> of your product.
3) Draw some <u>conclusions</u> from your testing and use these to explain how you'd <u>improve</u> your product.
4) Make sure you <u>explain things clearly</u> — get someone who knows nothing about your project to read it and see if it <u>makes sense</u>.
5) Examiners love it when you use the right <u>technical words</u>
   — they love it even more when you spell them correctly.

But Don't Forget The Exams — They're Worth 40%

1) There are two exams where you'll be tested on <u>everything</u> you've learned during the course — materials, tools, how to design things, how to make things, health and safety, environmental issues...
2) This book can help you <u>learn all that stuff</u> — and it has <u>questions</u> for you to <u>check</u> what you know.
3) There's a <u>glossary</u> at the back of the book, in case you need to sort out your mock-ups from your models.
4) The <u>exam technique</u> section (pages 78-81) has some <u>worked examples</u> of exam-style questions, and some hints on how to make sure you get <u>top marks</u>.

Evaluate, evaluate, evaluate...

When you evaluate a design or product, remember to explain which aspects of the design or product need <u>changing</u> and <u>why</u>. It's another little step on the long and winding road to coursework heaven.

New Product Design

Designers are influenced by loads of different factors when they work on a new product. The changing tastes of <u>customers</u>, the onward march of <u>technology</u>, and the increasing importance of <u>environmental concerns</u> are three big ones.

New Products Are Designed For Different Reasons

There are several reasons why a new product might be designed:

Market Pull is about what consumers want

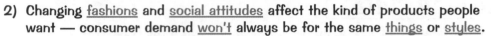

1) Designers <u>design stuff</u> (and manufacturers make it) to satisfy the <u>wants</u> and <u>needs</u> of consumers — consumer demand. Market pull is when new or improved products are designed as a result of consumer demand.

2) Changing <u>fashions</u> and <u>social attitudes</u> affect the kind of products people want — consumer demand <u>won't</u> always be for the same <u>things</u> or <u>styles</u>.

3) An example of where <u>market pull</u> has influenced the design of a graphic product is the <u>carrier bag</u>. It used to be simply a way to carry your shopping around, but now <u>consumers</u> expect it to reflect the <u>style</u> of the shop it comes from — and to take into account <u>environmental concerns</u>.

Bill was a consumer in dire need of a new razor.

Technology Push is about what manufacturers can provide

1) In industry, research and development departments are always coming up with <u>new technologies</u>, <u>materials</u> and <u>manufacturing techniques</u>. This can drive the design of new products.

2) <u>Manufacturers</u> can <u>use new technology</u> to <u>develop new products</u>, or to <u>improve existing ones</u>.

3) Using new technology might make an existing product <u>cheaper</u>, <u>better</u> at its <u>function</u> or <u>nicer-looking</u> — all things which will make products <u>easier to sell</u>.

4) The invention of <u>smart materials</u> is a <u>technology push</u> (see p. 28-29). E.g. <u>thermochromic inks</u> that change colour according to temperature have been used to create <u>drinks cans</u> that tell you when your drink is <u>nicely chilled</u>.

Designers have to think about the Environment

1) Designers now have to look at the impact their <u>designs</u> have on the <u>environment</u>.

2) Pressure comes from <u>customers</u> — who want to buy products that aren't wasteful and damaging, and from the <u>Government</u> — who try to make sure the manufacturing industry isn't being wasteful.

3) Packaging design has changed:

©1996 FSC A.C.

<u>Biodegradable plastics</u> are now being used for things like sandwich packaging.

Paper can be made from timber sourced from <u>responsibly managed</u> forests — the <u>Forest Stewardship Council</u> certifies products to show this.

4) Even <u>inks</u> can now be eco-friendly and sustainable, e.g. <u>vegetable-based</u> inks are made from a renewable resource (one that won't run out) and also release fewer <u>environmentally damaging</u> gases than petroleum-based inks.

Market Pull? I'm here for some lamb chops...

Being a designer means being aware of all this stuff. New products are coming out all the time, and old ones are constantly being updated to appeal to new customers. It's a <u>non-stop process</u>.

New Product Design

Good Design and Good Manufacture are Different

A well-designed product won't necessarily be well-manufactured and vice versa.

A well-designed product:

- can carry out its <u>function</u> really well
- <u>looks</u> good and attracts consumers

A well-manufactured product:

- has been <u>made</u> to a <u>good standard</u> — things like the finish, folds, colour and material are all satisfactory
- is <u>accurate</u> to the original design

1) The quality of the <u>materials</u> used in making the product are really important. A brilliantly designed poster printed on poor quality paper won't look as good as one printed on higher quality paper.

2) The different <u>methods</u> used in production have a big impact on the final product. Printing a flier on a cheap home inkjet printer won't look as good as one done by a professional printer using lithography.

3) If you're getting a product printed by someone else, always ask for a <u>proof</u> — this is a <u>single copy</u> produced to show you <u>exactly</u> what your product will look like if it's put into production.

Good Design and Product Choice Improves Lives

1) Good design can improve people's <u>quality of life</u> — it can actually make life better. E.g. some people want a clock that looks <u>really trendy</u>, some people just want one that's <u>cheap</u> but does the job, whereas my Gran wants one with <u>nice big numbers</u> so she can read it easily.

2) Harry Beck's London Underground map design has made it easier for people to get around London, by making the Underground system easier to understand.

3) <u>Competition</u> between different companies often encourages <u>good design</u>. If there was only one company making a product they may not be as keen to <u>constantly improve</u> things to make the best possible product.

4) A wide range of competing designs give consumers more <u>choice</u> — for example, there wouldn't be such a big choice of greetings cards if there was only one company making them.

5) Competition tends to make products <u>cheaper</u>. Companies try to design products that will be cheaper than their competitors'. For example, MP3 players have become a lot cheaper since lots of different companies started making them.

Practice Questions

1) What is meant by <u>market pull</u>?

2) Give an example of a product that has been introduced because of <u>technology push</u>.

3) Paul is designing a birthday card.
   Suggest <u>two things</u> he could do to make it more <u>environmentally friendly</u>.

4) Helen is designing a new <u>diary</u>.
   Helen looks at the <u>design</u> and <u>manufacture</u> of some existing products.
   a) Suggest two features of a <u>well-designed</u> diary.
   b) Suggest two features of a <u>well-manufactured</u> diary.

Design and The Target Group

When you're designing a product, you have to think about the <u>people</u> you're designing it <u>for</u> — in other words, your <u>target group</u>. At the end of the day they're the ones you've got to <u>impress</u>.

Find a Gap in the Market...

1) The design process often starts when someone finds a <u>gap in the market</u>. This is an area where there aren't products available to meet <u>people's needs</u>. For example, there aren't many <u>pop-up recipe books</u>.

2) The next stage is to hire a <u>designer</u> — and they design a <u>new product</u> to fill the gap.

3) The new product then needs to be <u>manufactured</u> and <u>sold</u>. Simple.

Tim's Mum had to tell him there weren't any pop-up recipe books available.

...And Decide Who Your Target Group is

It's important to work out what group of people you want to sell your product to — the <u>target market</u>. You can group people by things like <u>age</u>, <u>gender</u>, <u>job</u>, <u>hobbies</u>, <u>how rich they are</u>...

> For example... the target market for <u>pop-up recipe books</u> is probably the <u>parents</u> of <u>young children</u> who are <u>interested in cooking</u>.

1) You need to <u>design</u> the product with the target group in mind...

2) ...and aim your <u>marketing</u> (advertising, free samples, etc) at them.

Once you've chosen your target group, you've got to go about designing a <u>great product</u> — to do that, you've got to consider <u>ergonomics</u> and <u>anthropometrics</u>...

Ergonomic Designs Are Easy for People to Use

Good design includes making a product <u>easy</u> and <u>comfortable</u> for people to use — this is <u>ergonomics</u>.

1) **LETTERING** must be easy for the <u>target market</u> to <u>read</u>. For example, lettering for older people should not be too small, and the typeface for children's books should be especially large and clear.

2) Use **COLOUR** to achieve the effect you want (see p. 43). <u>Complementary colours</u> will make something <u>stand out</u>. Avoid relying on a contrast between red and green though — it won't be very clear for people who have red/green colour-blindness (the commonest kind). And if you want your design to be <u>easy on the eye</u>, use colours that are <u>close together</u> on the colour wheel.

3) Products must be the right **SIZE AND SHAPE** for the intended users — see the next page.

4) If part of the product needs to be <u>gripped</u>, the **TEXTURE** might be important.

5) If the product needs to be <u>carried</u> or <u>moved</u> you'll need to keep its **WEIGHT** down by choosing the right <u>materials</u>.

My target group would be Take That...

To summarise: 1) find a <u>gap</u> in the market, 2) decide who your <u>target group</u> is, 3) design a product that will <u>appeal</u> to that target group and is <u>easy and comfortable</u> to use, 4) bask in your new-found <u>wealth</u>.

Design and The Target Group

Anthropometric Data are Measurements of Humans

To make your product the right size, you need to know the likely body measurements of the users.
Measurements of human body parts are called anthropometric data.

1) First, work out what measurements you need. For example, if your product is a novelty mask
   it doesn't matter how long the users' legs are — you only need to know about their heads.

2) Find out what these measurements are on the typical user of the product.
   (The best way is to sample lots of people from the target group then take the average.)

3) Design your product to fit someone with these average measurements.

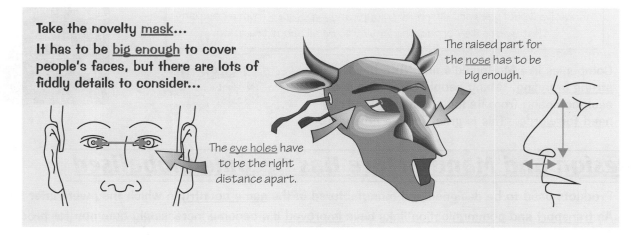

Take the novelty mask...
It has to be big enough to cover
people's faces, but there are lots of
fiddly details to consider...

The eye holes have
to be the right
distance apart.

The raised part for
the nose has to be
big enough.

4) BUT a product that fits only the average person isn't the best solution (most people aren't average).

5) So designers often aim to make the product fit okay for 90% of the target users.
   For example, they'd make the nose of the mask bigger than needed for the average nose.

Practice Questions

1) What is meant by a gap in the market?

2) a) What is a target group?
   b) Ryan is designing a 'Learn Your Alphabet' toy.
      What kind of people do you think should be his target group?

3) Sally has designed a brochure for her school open day.
   She wants her design to be ergonomic.
   a) What is an ergonomic design?
   b) Suggest two things she should think about.

4) a) What is anthropometric data?
   b) Suggest what anthropometric data would be needed for designing a T-shirt.

5) Calum has designed a drink-dispensing top hat to fit 90% of his target group.
   Explain why he hasn't just used the average measurements of his target group.

Making and Selling Products

Companies try to build up a <u>corporate identity</u> — the company's <u>personality</u>, <u>style</u> and <u>brand</u>.

Strong Corporate Identity Includes Brand Recognition

1) <u>Memorable graphics</u> are a really good way to make sure that consumers <u>recognise</u> your products, e.g. using a <u>logo</u>. Many companies often apply their logo and colour scheme to all <u>printed material</u> (e.g. business cards, letterheads and compliments slips) as well as their <u>products</u>, <u>packaging</u>, <u>uniforms</u> and <u>transport</u>.

2) <u>Well designed</u> graphics should help the company to get its message across, or build up its <u>corporate identity</u> — the image it wants people to have of the company.

> For example, a company that wants people to think of it as modern and creative would use very different <u>colours</u> and <u>typefaces</u> from a company that wants its corporate identity to be all about tradition.

3) Companies like McDonald's and NIKE have <u>strong branding</u>. Many people can recognise each company from its logo alone, <u>without the need for words</u>. This is great for the company.

EXAM TIP
You might have to design a logo in the exam.

Design and Manufacture Has Become Globalised

1) Products used to be designed and manufactured in the <u>same country</u> in which they were later sold.

2) As <u>transport</u> and <u>communication links</u> have <u>improved</u> it's become increasingly common for products to be manufactured in one country and sold in another. This is known as <u>globalisation</u>.

3) Some products are made in <u>more than one</u> country — their various components are made all over the world and then assembled in one place.

4) The globalisation of products has advantages and disadvantages:

Advantages
- Production <u>costs less</u> as it can take place in countries where <u>materials</u>, <u>wages</u> and <u>energy</u> are <u>cheap</u>.
- The savings made during production may be passed on to the <u>consumer</u> as <u>lower prices</u>.
- Customers have greater <u>product choice</u> — they can use the internet to buy products from all over the world.
- Manufacturers can make more money as they have a <u>worldwide customer-base</u>.

Disadvantages
- More <u>energy</u> is used and more <u>pollution</u> is created through <u>transporting</u> materials, parts and finished products from country to country.
- Designing can become more <u>complicated</u> — products designed to be sold worldwide need to take into account many different <u>cultures</u>, be suitable for different <u>power sources</u> and may need to have instructions in <u>different languages</u>.
- Some people think that globalisation <u>reduces</u> the <u>variety of designs</u>, with products from different cultures becoming more and more similar.

Look, it's Russell — ooh, and there's Jo...

Nothing ever stays the same. Even classic designs get <u>adapted</u> and <u>updated</u> over the years. Which is lucky for you designer-types as it means you'll be able to get jobs putting <u>cool new stuff</u> together.

Making and Selling Products

Some Products Have _Obsolescence_ Built In

If the stuff you bought <u>lasted forever</u>, there'd be no more jobs for designers and manufacturers.
Luckily for them, that's not how it works. That product life-cycle just <u>keeps on going</u>, because:

1) Many products do eventually <u>break</u>.

2) Other products become so <u>out of date</u> that you <u>can't use them</u> (computers that are incompatible with new software, say) or you <u>don't want to</u> (because everyone else has newer, better stuff).

3) This stage — when a product is useless and the consumer <u>has to replace</u> it — is called <u>obsolescence</u>.

4) Sometimes designers <u>deliberately</u> design stuff so that it'll become useless quite quickly.
This is called <u>built-in obsolescence</u>. Here are some ways to do it.

- Make the design <u>poor quality</u> — so the product breaks quickly.
- Design the product so it's <u>impossible</u> or <u>really expensive</u> to <u>repair</u> or <u>update</u>.
- Make the design really <u>up to the minute</u> — so that it's bound to become <u>unfashionable</u> quickly.

This has _Advantages_ and _Disadvantages_

<u>On the plus side:</u>

Built-in obsolescence drives <u>innovation</u> in new replacement products, and keeps designers and manufacturers in <u>jobs</u>.

I've only had this calendar a year, and now it doesn't work <u>at all</u>...

<u>But, then again...</u>

Your <u>customers</u> might just get <u>annoyed</u> if they have to replace the product really soon, and never buy anything from you again.

Also, it's not great for the <u>environment</u>. You end up with mountains of <u>thrown away</u> products. And making all the replacement products uses up more <u>resources</u> and <u>energy</u> and often causes more <u>pollution</u>.

Practice Questions

1) Alex employed a graphic designer to come up with this <u>logo</u> for his coffee shop.
   a) Why do companies often use a logo?
   b) In what ways is the logo effective?

2) a) What is meant by the term <u>globalisation</u>?
   b) Name <u>two factors</u> that have helped lead to globalisation.
   c) Give <u>two advantages</u> and <u>two disadvantages</u> of globalisation.

3) Julie has designed a board game with <u>built-in obsolescence</u>.
   a) What is meant by built-in obsolescence?
   b) Suggest some features that Julie's design could have to give it built-in obsolescence.
   c) Give one <u>advantage</u> and one <u>disadvantage</u> of built-in obsolescence.

Life-Cycle and Carbon Footprint

Designers need to consider the environmental impact of a product's <u>whole life</u> — including the <u>materials</u> and <u>processes</u> used in production, the effect of <u>using</u> the product and finally <u>disposing</u> of it.

Ecodesign Considers a Product's Environmental Impact

1) The environmental impact of a product over its <u>entire life-cycle</u> is known as its <u>eco-footprint</u>.
2) Environmentally friendly products are becoming popular — many consumers are put off buying products that <u>waste resources</u> or can't be <u>recycled</u>.
3) <u>Eco-design</u> involves making products that are <u>sustainable</u>. Sustainability means not causing <u>permanent damage</u> to the environment and not using up <u>finite resources</u> (ones that'll eventually run out).

If you're going to be an <u>eco-designer</u>, one thing you'll have to do is...

Carry Out a Life-Cycle Analysis

It's sometimes called a Life Cycle <u>Assessment</u>.

A <u>life-cycle analysis (LCA)</u> looks at each <u>stage</u> of the <u>life</u> of a product — from the raw materials to when it's disposed of. It works out the potential <u>environmental impact</u>:

Choice of material

1) <u>Hardwoods</u> are often obtained from natural <u>rainforests</u>. Felling the trees destroys the habitat of pretty much everything living there (including people). <u>Softwoods</u> are a <u>greener choice</u>. They're usually from <u>managed plantations</u> — so more trees are planted and grow quickly to replace them. <u>Recycled</u> wood is also a good choice for the environment.
2) <u>Paper and card</u> can be made from <u>recycled fibres</u> — it's often impossible to tell recycled stuff apart from the stuff made from fresh wood pulp.
3) <u>Metals</u> have to be <u>mined</u> and <u>extracted</u> from their ores. Most <u>plastics</u> are made using <u>crude oil</u>, which is a <u>finite resource</u>. These processes need a lot of <u>energy</u> and cause a lot of <u>pollution</u>.

Some products can be <u>recycled</u> — the materials can be used again in new products.

Manufacture

1) <u>Manufacturing</u> products uses a lot of <u>energy</u> and other resources. It can also cause a lot of <u>pollution</u>.
2) Producing recycled paper is more <u>energy efficient</u> and causes <u>less air pollution</u> than making new paper.
3) You also need to think about <u>waste</u> material and how to <u>dispose</u> of it.

Product Disposal

1) Products are often <u>disposed</u> of in a <u>landfill</u> site at the end of their life.
2) This takes up space and <u>pollutes</u> land and water (e.g. when paint washes off a product and gets into rivers).

Using the product

<u>Using</u> the product can also damage the environment. E.g. <u>electrical products</u> use electricity generated by burning <u>fossil fuels</u>, and <u>paint</u> can give off <u>toxic fumes</u>.

Make sure your product's footprint isn't a pair of size 12s...

In the last few years, consumers have become far more <u>aware</u> of issues like these. As a result, many <u>manufacturers</u> have started to clean up their act and tried to <u>reduce</u> their <u>environmental impact</u>.

Life-Cycle and Carbon Footprint

Products have a Carbon Footprint

1) A <u>carbon footprint</u> is the amount of <u>greenhouse gases</u> (carbon dioxide, methane and other gases) released by doing or making something.

> Greenhouse gases are gases that contribute to the <u>greenhouse effect</u>. They limit how much heat can escape from the Earth's atmosphere — releasing lots of these gases is causing the planet's <u>temperature</u> to <u>rise</u>.

2) <u>All</u> products have a carbon footprint — because <u>carbon dioxide</u> is released when they're <u>made</u>, <u>transported</u> and often when they're <u>used</u>. That's because <u>fossil fuels</u> are burned to provide the <u>energy</u> for these processes, and this emits carbon dioxide.

3) So the more <u>energy</u> that's needed to make something, the <u>bigger</u> its carbon footprint.

4) <u>A lot</u> of <u>energy</u> is used to <u>manufacture plastics</u>, so plastic products have a <u>huge</u> carbon footprint.

5) A product's carbon footprint is also affected by the distance it travels from where it's <u>made</u> to where it's <u>used</u> (this is called <u>product miles</u>).

6) Making products so that they <u>use energy efficiently</u> could <u>reduce</u> their carbon footprint. Lots of appliances now have efficiency ratings, e.g. an A-rated fridge is more efficient than a D-rated one.

Carbon Emissions Can Be Offset

Everything from lighting a building to transporting people or goods has a <u>carbon footprint</u>. To reduce the <u>impact</u> something has on the <u>environment</u>, some of its carbon emissions can be <u>offset</u> (i.e. reduced in another area).

CARBON OFFSETTING

1) Both <u>individuals</u> and <u>companies</u> can offset their carbon dioxide emissions.

2) Offsetting means <u>donating money</u> to projects that <u>reduce</u> carbon emissions — to <u>balance out</u> the greenhouse gases you're responsible for. These emissions are calculated by carbon offsetting companies.

3) Projects include <u>planting trees</u>, investing in wind and solar power, and recycling projects.

Practice Questions

1) a) What is meant by the term <u>eco-design</u>?
   b) What does the term <u>sustainable</u> mean?

2) a) What is a <u>life-cycle analysis</u>?
   b) What are the <u>four stages</u> of a life-cycle analysis?

3) a) What is a <u>carbon footprint</u>?
   b) Explain why <u>all products</u> have a carbon footprint.
   c) Suggest <u>one</u> way in which a product's carbon footprint might be <u>reduced</u>.

4) Briefly describe how a company might <u>offset</u> their carbon emissions.

Product Research

Designers don't just pluck design ideas out of the air — they often <u>analyse</u> similar <u>existing products</u> first.

Determine the Function of a Product

> **FUNCTION AND FITNESS FOR PURPOSE:**
> <u>Function</u> is the job a product is <u>intended</u> to do.
> <u>Fitness for purpose</u> is whether the product does its job well or not.

You'll have to do all this stuff for your controlled assessments.

1) You can only really tell if a product is fit for purpose by actually <u>using it</u>.
2) For example, a menu holder may look fantastic in a picture on the <u>internet</u>, but if you actually <u>use it</u> you may find it doesn't securely hold a menu and breaks if you try to put more than one menu in it.
3) If a product does work well, try to <u>work out</u> what makes it good, and if there's anything about it that you could <u>adapt</u> for your own designs.
4) If it <u>doesn't</u> work so well then work out how you could <u>improve</u> it.

Look at a Range of Similar Products

> **COMPETITION AND COST:** You need to consider <u>value for money</u>.
> For example, if you're looking at a <u>CD storage case</u>, find out whether it's cheaper or more expensive than <u>similar</u> CD storage cases. You'll also need to look at <u>how it performs</u> and <u>looks</u> compared to these other storage cases.

1) By looking at a range of products you can combine all the <u>best bits</u> from them to use in your ideas.
2) For example, you may like the <u>shape</u> of one product, the <u>materials</u> of another, and so on.
3) You could also look at things which do a <u>similar job</u>. If you're making a magazine rack — look at CD racks, wine bottle racks, and toast racks to get ideas.

Work Out How it's Made

> **MANUFACTURING METHODS:**
> It's important to try and work out how a product has been <u>made</u> when you analyse it.

Cyril concluded that the tomatoes had been glued to the pizza base using cheese.

1) <u>Disassembling</u> (taking apart) a product can help you find out <u>how it was made</u>. For example, has it been glued together? Has it been laminated?
2) Make careful notes as you disassemble something, and record what <u>component parts</u> have been used and how it's <u>structured</u>, using <u>sketches</u> or <u>photos</u>.
3) Ask yourself why the designers have made the <u>decisions</u> they have — every method has different <u>strengths</u> and <u>weaknesses</u>. Try to work out if they made the decisions for cost, appearance, strength, or a combination of all of these factors.
4) See if you could use any of the methods for your <u>own</u> design. For example, if you're looking at product packaging boxes, take a look at different net designs — see if you can adapt them for the product packaging <u>you're designing</u>.

A dolphin work-out — fitness for porpoise...

This is where the real hands-on research gets underway. Get that product, hold it in your hands, smell it, turn it upside-down. Identify the <u>top-notch products</u> and the ones that designers got wrong.

Product Research

Decide if it's Innovative

INNOVATION: This means a product doing something clever in a way that hasn't been done before.

1) Every now and then a really innovative product comes along...
   The upside-down sauce bottle is an innovative product. Not long ago you had to shake sauce bottles to get the sauce out — this was slow and messy. Upside-down bottles solved this problem by putting the bottle cap where the sauce was — at the bottom of the bottle.

2) If you find a boring, run-of-the-mill product that isn't at all innovative, think about improvements you could make.

Work Out if it's Environmentally Friendly

EXAM TIP
One of the papers is all about sustainability so you're bound to be asked about this stuff.

ECO-FOOTPRINT AND SUSTAINABILITY: When analysing products it's really important to think about their impact on the environment.

1) Nowadays, designers and manufacturers need to do all they can to make their products as environmentally friendly as possible.

2) So when you're analysing a product, look at things like —
   • power — Does it use rechargeable batteries, wind-up power, disposable batteries, or something else?
   • materials — Are they recyclable? Do they come from a finite source (like oil)? Does the product contain unnecessary material?

3) Suggest improvements that could make the product more environmentally friendly. For example — "The Happy Birthday banner would be better if it was made from organic cotton rather than PVC. Also, the flashing LED lights could be solar powered rather than battery operated."

Practice Questions

1) What is meant by the following terms:
   a) function?
   b) fitness for purpose?

2) Clive is designing a photo album. He starts by looking at some existing products.
   a) Why is this a good idea?
   b) Suggest another similar product he could look at to get ideas from.
   c) How could disassembling another photo album help him?

3) Name one example of an innovative product. Explain why it's innovative.

4) Jenny is making a point of sale display.
   She decides to make it out of corrugated plastic and includes a waving clown that is battery operated.
   Suggest two things she could do to make her stand more environmentally friendly.

Task Analysis

The best products are those that address a real need. The more people there are who would actually use a product, the more chance it stands of being a roaring success.

Designing Starts with the Design Brief

When someone gets an idea for a new product, they often employ a designer to work on the idea.

1) The person who hires the designer is called the client.

2) The client gives the designer a design brief...

3) The design brief is a starting point for the development of the product. It will probably include:

> • what kind of product is needed (and why)
> • how the product will be used
> • who the product is for (the target market)

DESIGN BRIEF FOR STAPLE PACKAGING/WOODLOUSE HOUSE

No currently commercially available staple packaging has an in-built capacity for housing a pet woodlouse.
We want you to design a product to meet this need for those people who want to keep a pet after they've stapled their papers.

4) When the designer gets the design brief they'll start by analysing it — making sure they understand what the client wants.

5) Then they'll do lots of research.

In industry, the client supplies the design brief. In the exam, the examiner gives you a brief...

You'll Need to Do Some Research...

As well as analysing existing products (see pages 12-13), designers need to research the potential market for the product. This is called market research.

1) The point of doing market research is to:

> • find out what people like or dislike about similar existing products
> • check that people will actually want your product

2) Even the best products won't be everyone's cup of tea — some people will like them and some won't.

3) Ask your target market what they want the product to be like.

4) You can ask closed questions, e.g. 'Which of these three fonts do you like best?'

5) Or you can ask open questions, e.g. 'Why is Comic Sans MS your favourite font?'
(This kind of question is good if you want to get more detail about people's opinions.)

...And Use Your Research to Draw Conclusions

Once you've done some product analysis and market research, you should have loads of information. Now you have to use the information to help with your design.

> 1) Summarise what you've found out — pick out the most important and useful findings.
> E.g. 70% of people found it difficult to read text printed in size 10 Times New Roman font.
>
> 2) Explain what impact the research will have on your designs.
> E.g. the font on my design should be size 12 or bigger.

This will help you write a design specification — see the next page...

Draw conclusions with research — not a pencil...

The rest of this section describes the typical design process that happens in industry. You need to understand the overall process even though you probably won't have to actually do every bit of it.

Task Analysis

The Design Specification is a List of Conditions to Meet

1) The design specification gives certain <u>conditions</u> that the product must meet.
These conditions should take account of your <u>research findings</u>.

> E.g. if you know that your target market would never buy a
> box of staples that costs more than £100, your design specification
> might include the statement, "Must cost £100 or less."

2) It's best to write a specification as <u>bullet points</u> rather than a paragraph of explanations.
Include points to describe <u>some</u> or <u>all</u> of the following:

1. How it should look	4. Size
2. How it will be used	5. Safety points to consider
3. Materials, equipment and production method	6. Price range

Example:
- The packaging should weigh 80 g or less.
- It should be multicoloured.
- The maximum length will be 100 mm.
- The font should be size 12 or bigger.

3) The design specification acts as a <u>guide</u> to make sure that the product
will do what you want it to — you <u>refer back to it</u> throughout the project.

4) So it's important that it's <u>clear and detailed</u> — the better it is, the more
likely your product will be high quality.

5) Once you've got your design specification, it's time to start coming up
with <u>design ideas</u> (see the next page...).

Practice Questions

1) a) What information does a <u>design brief</u> include?
   b) In industry, who <u>writes</u> the design brief?

2) What's the point of doing <u>market research</u>?

3) Read these questionnaire results about fonts and write two brief <u>conclusions</u> based on them:

> Q1. Which colour font do you think the text looks best in?
> Answers: red: **9**   black: **18**   blue: **24**   green: **6**
> Q2. Do you think the size of the font is too small?
> Answers: yes: **42**   no: **15**

4) a) What is a <u>design specification</u>?
   b) List some things that a design specification should include.
   c) Write a design specification for a <u>display stand</u> for a new chocolate bar.

Generating Proposals

When you're coming up with ideas for products, try to be as <u>adventurous</u> and <u>creative</u> as possible.

There are a Few Tricks That Can Help You Get Started

1) Create a <u>mood board</u> — a load of different images, words, materials, colours...
2) <u>Brainstorm</u> — think up key words, questions and initial thoughts relating to your product. Start off by just writing whatever ideas come into your head and analyse them later.
3) Work from an <u>existing product</u> — but change some of its features or production methods so that it fits in with your <u>specification</u>.

Don't Just Go With the First Thing You Think Of

You need to produce a <u>wide range</u> of different <u>design ideas</u>.

1) <u>Annotate</u> (add <u>notes</u> to) each idea to explain it fully.

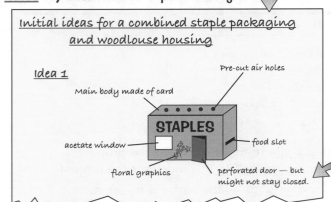

Initial ideas for a combined staple packaging and woodlouse housing

Idea 1

Pre-cut air holes

Main body made of card

STAPLES

acetate window

floral graphics

food slot

perforated door — but might not stay closed.

EXAM TIP
Your initial ideas should be sketched freehand in pencil fairly quickly.

When you're annotating your designs, don't just describe what you've drawn. It's a good idea to <u>evaluate</u> the design too and include <u>critical comments</u>.

2) Once you've got a few possible designs, you need to <u>check</u> that each one <u>matches</u> your <u>specification</u> — any that don't <u>won't</u> be <u>suitable</u>.
3) Also, check that you <u>could actually make</u> the designs. <u>Creativity</u> is a <u>splendid</u> thing... ...but total impracticality isn't.
4) Finally, choose <u>one</u> of your suitable designs to <u>develop further</u>.

Social and Cultural Differences Affect Designing

1) An example of a <u>cultural difference</u> is different ways of <u>eating</u>. Traditionally, Japanese people eat at a low table sitting on the floor. So products aimed at the Japanese market that feature <u>images of people eating</u> should reflect this.
2) <u>Dress</u> also differs between cultures. For example, a <u>promotional vest-top</u> would be fine in Western cultures, but wouldn't go down well in Islamic cultures where modest dress is expected.
3) Culture can also affect <u>aesthetic</u> qualities (looks). Some cultures are associated with particular patterns or colours, e.g. <u>green</u> is often associated with <u>Islam</u> — and also with <u>Ireland</u>.

I bet your mood is bored at the moment...

There's a lot to <u>think about</u> when you're designing — but don't let that put you off. Remember, it should be <u>fun</u> too. It's important to take into account how <u>other people</u> might view your design though.

Generating Proposals

Cultural differences aren't the only things to bear in mind when you're coming up with designs...

Designers Must Be Aware of the Feelings of Others

Designers need to be sensitive to the feelings of different groups in society.

1) They need to make sure that designs do not put off, insult or offend people for political, religious, gender or cultural reasons.

2) Certain symbols are almost certain to offend some people no matter how they're used, e.g. a swastika.

3) Other symbolism will offend people if they believe it's been misused or abused. This is especially true for religious symbols.

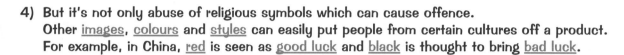

4) But it's not only abuse of religious symbols which can cause offence. Other images, colours and styles can easily put people from certain cultures off a product. For example, in China, red is seen as good luck and black is thought to bring bad luck.

Carol's Comics
— so simple, even a woman can understand them.

This sort of thing might have appeared in the 1920s...

...but you mightn't get away with it today.

5) Sexism and racism, either in text or in images, is sure to offend loads of people.

6) Some people are offended by images containing nudity and violence.

7) It's impossible to list everything that could cause someone, somewhere offence. Designers just have to try and put themselves in other people's shoes, and imagine how they might feel when they see the design.

Practice Questions

1) James is stuck for design ideas for a limited edition DVD case.
   a) What three things could he do to get his creative juices flowing?
   b) Sketch three design ideas for the DVD case, including annotation.

2) Name a product where the design might be affected by culture.

3) Give an example of a design that might offend people and explain why this is offensive.

Creative juices come in different flavours.

4) John is designing a set of key fobs.
   a) Sketch a design for a key fob that might appeal to a very patriotic British person.
   b) Explain why John might avoid using a cross on his designs.

5) Give one example of how a particular colour might appeal to people from a certain background.

Development

There's only so much <u>development</u> you can do <u>on paper</u>. Making <u>mock-ups</u>, <u>models</u> and <u>prototypes</u> of your product means that you can <u>test</u>, <u>evaluate</u> and <u>modify</u> the design.

Different Sorts of Model are Used at Different Stages

Not that kind...

Models can be <u>2D or 3D drawings</u> done by hand or using CAD (page 72) — in 3D CAD packages you can view your design from <u>all angles</u>. Or you could actually <u>make</u> 3D models, maybe <u>scaled down</u> in size, to check the shape of your design.

Mock-ups are usually <u>full-scale</u> and made of <u>cheap</u> paper and card. A full scale mock-up will help you check that your design is <u>ergonomic</u>. You might also use a mock-up to quickly check the construction of <u>nets</u>, or for a <u>magazine</u> or <u>menu</u> design to check the colours and images.

Prototypes are <u>mock-ups</u> that are exactly the same as the finished product will be. They include all the <u>components</u> and <u>mechanisms</u>, and they're made using the right <u>materials</u> and <u>construction</u> methods.

See below for more on prototypes.

Models and Mock-Ups are Used to Improve the Design

Making models and mock-ups is a good way to spot and solve <u>problems</u>.

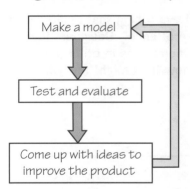

Make a model → Test and evaluate → Come up with ideas to improve the product

1) You can make models using materials that are <u>easy</u> and <u>quick</u> to work with, e.g. <u>cardboard</u>, <u>balsa wood</u> or <u>expanded polystyrene</u>.
2) After you've made each model, do some <u>tests</u> to check that it works how it's supposed to.
3) You should also <u>evaluate</u> each model against the <u>design specification</u>. Take each point and see if your model is up to scratch.
4) There are probably some things that <u>don't work out</u> quite how you'd hoped. <u>Write down</u> what the problem is, suggest how to <u>fix it</u> and make another model.
5) Record how the design develops — <u>take photos</u> of your models.

Prototypes Help Manufacturers Avoid Big Mistakes

A lot of <u>money</u> is at stake when new products are introduced. Making a <u>prototype</u> before the final <u>industrial production</u> helps ensure that money isn't <u>wasted</u>.

1) You can <u>test</u> that the product <u>works</u> properly and is <u>safe</u>.
2) You can ask potential <u>end-users</u> (customers) for <u>feedback</u>, to see whether the product <u>meets their needs</u>.
3) If the prototype <u>works well</u> and potential customers <u>like it</u>, a manufacturer would consider going into production on a <u>larger scale</u>.

The final product you make for your first controlled assessment is a prototype of your design.

A good model — serious expression, striking a pose...

Models are <u>really important</u> in design. It'd be a <u>bad idea</u> to go straight from the 2D drawings to making <u>zillions</u> of the final product — lots of potential problems are <u>ironed out</u> during the modelling stage.

Development

You might think your design is the best thing since sliced bread, but your opinion isn't the only one that counts (after all, you probably won't be buying that many of your product)...

Consult Other People About Your Design

1) Find out people's opinions about your various models.
2) This will help you refine your ideas so you can arrive at the best solution.
3) Relevant market research questions might include:

- Do you find the text easy to read?
- Do you like the colours?
- What is the most striking feature?
- What don't you like about the product?
- How much would you be willing to pay?

So would you consider buying one?

Now You Should Know Exactly What You're Making

Once you've finished developing your ideas and have a final design, you should have worked out:

1) The best materials, tools and other equipment to use (and their availability).
2) The approximate manufacturing time needed to make each item.
3) How much it should cost to manufacture each item.
   If you were making items on a large scale, the energy costs (e.g. for electricity to run the printer) would be significant, so they'd need to be factored in too.
4) The assembly process — this is important when it comes to planning production (see next page).

Practice Questions

1) Laura wants to make a scaled down 3D model of her design for a clock.
   a) Suggest some materials she could use for the model.
   b) What should Laura use the model for?

2) What is the difference between a mock-up and a prototype?

3) Doris has designed some weighing scales. She has made a prototype of her design. Describe how Doris could use the prototype to help her decide whether to go into larger scale production.

4) Zara is designing birthday cards.
   a) She has made mock-ups of some pop-up birthday cards. She plans to do some market research. Suggest four market research questions she could ask about her mock-up cards.
   b) Zara has finished the final design for her birthday cards.
      Suggest four things she should have worked out by this stage.

Planning Production

In industry, designers usually just <u>design</u> things — they don't make them as well.
So they have to tell the <u>manufacturer</u> exactly <u>what</u> the product is and <u>how</u> to make it.

You Need to Produce a Manufacturing Specification

A manufacturing specification can be a <u>series of written statements</u>, or <u>working drawings</u> and <u>sequence diagrams</u> (see next page). It has to explain <u>exactly</u> how to make the product, and should include:

1) <u>clear construction details</u> explaining <u>exactly</u> how to make each part,

2) <u>materials</u> — which materials to use for each part and how much will be needed,

3) <u>sizes</u> — <u>precise measurements</u> of each part in <u>millimetres</u>,

4) <u>tolerances</u> — the maximum and minimum sizes each part should be,

5) <u>finishing</u> details — any special information, such as 'laminate the paper with aluminium',

6) <u>quality control</u> instructions — when and how checks should be made.

7) <u>costings</u> — how much each part costs, and details of any other costs involved.

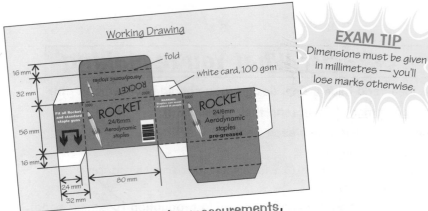

Working drawings give <u>measurements</u>, <u>materials</u> and <u>construction</u> details
(e.g. where to make folds).

<u>Spreadsheets</u> are great for
working out <u>costings</u>.

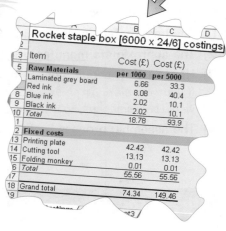

Plan Each Stage in Detail

Take <u>each stage</u> of the process and plan it <u>in detail</u>. You also need to think about:

1) <u>how long</u> each stage will take,

2) what needs to be <u>prepared</u> before you can start each stage,

3) how you will <u>ensure consistency</u> and <u>quality</u>,

4) how you will do <u>quality control checks</u>,

5) what <u>health and safety precautions</u> you will have to take.

Remember, your <u>methods</u> would probably <u>change</u> if you were going to produce your design in <u>quantity</u>. (In your projects, you should definitely write about <u>how</u> they'd change.)

Clear construction details — "Insert tab A into slot B"*

You know what they say... the devil's in the detail. Yeah, well, I don't know exactly what that means, but it's probably something to do with being really precise. And that's what you've got to do with your manufacturer's specification, or your marvellous masterpiece could end up as a disastrous dog's dinner.

* ...which doesn't fit, so try it in every other slot before widening
slot B until it does actually fit. Repeat for tabs B, C and D.

Planning Production

Making a few examples of your product is (relatively) easy. But mass-producing it is a whole different ball game. And it takes a shed-load of careful planning.

(You can of course plan things <u>in a shed</u>, while <u>bouncing a ball</u> against the wall.)

Use <u>Charts</u> to Help You

You need to work out <u>what order</u> to do things in.

① **Work Order** This can be produced as a <u>table</u> or <u>flow chart</u>. The purpose of a work order is to plan the <u>sequence</u> of tasks to be carried out.
The work order could include details of tools and equipment, quality control stages, safety, and so on.

Prototype staple box			
<u>Day</u>	<u>Process</u>	<u>Tools needed</u>	<u>Quality ch</u>
1	Print designs	Airbrush, pens, dry transfer lettering	Make s
2	Cut out net	Scalpel, metal rule	Chec
	Score and fold net	Scissors, metal rule	

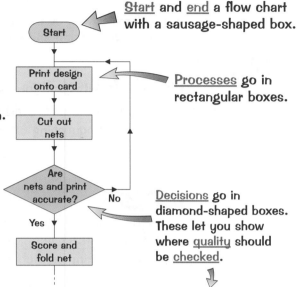

<u>Start</u> and <u>end</u> a flow chart with a sausage-shaped box.

<u>Processes</u> go in rectangular boxes.

<u>Decisions</u> go in diamond-shaped boxes. These let you show where <u>quality</u> should be <u>checked</u>.

The diamond shaped boxes show where you will stop and see if your product looks and works how it should. If you find it doesn't, go back and make sure it's done properly before you move on.

You also need to work out <u>how long</u> each stage will take, and how these times will fit into the <u>total time</u> you've allowed for production. One way to do this is with a Gantt chart:

② **Gantt Chart** The tasks are listed down the <u>left-hand</u> side, and the <u>timing</u> is plotted across the top. The coloured squares show <u>how long</u> each task takes, and the <u>order</u> they're done in.

	5 mins	10 mins	15 mins	20 mins	25 mins	30 mins	35 mins	40 mins	45 mins	50 mins	55 mins	60 mins	65 mins	70 mins	75 mins	80 mins	85 mins	90 mins	95 mins	100 mins
Mark out box and cutting template																				
Mask white areas, airbrush box																				
Allow paint to dry																				
Cut out cutting template																				
Apply writing																				
Outline logo with fine marker																				
Colour logo with paint or felt tips																				
Use template to cut box out																				
Mark out and score folds																				
Assemble box																				

You can start the next stage while the paint's drying, so draw the bars underneath each other.

Practice Questions

1) a) What is a <u>manufacturing specification</u>?
   b) List <u>three things</u> that a manufacturing specification might include.

2) What are <u>working drawings</u>?

3) On a flow chart, how would you show where <u>quality control</u> should take place?

4) Mike is making an <u>orange juice carton</u>. He has made a Gantt chart of the process.
   a) Why don't any of the bars <u>overlap</u>?
   b) How long does the <u>whole process</u> last?
   c) Which is the <u>longest stage</u>? How long does it last?

	5 mins	10 mins	15 mins	20 mins	25 mins	30 mins	35 mins	40 mins	45 mins	50 mins	55 mins	60 mins	65 mins	70 mins	75 mins	80 mins
Laminate paper with aluminium																
Cut out shape of carton																
Mask white areas, airbrush carton																
Allow paint to dry																
Apply writing and logo																
Mark and score folds																
Assemble carton																

Properties of Graphic Materials

You need to know about the different <u>materials</u> you could use for your graphic product —
and what <u>properties</u> they have.

Different Materials Have Different Properties

Make sure you're <u>really familiar</u> with all these terms — if you start getting strength and hardness mixed
up, or get confused about what tough and flexible mean, you'll be dropping marks all over the place.

STRENGTH

Strength is the ability to <u>withstand forces</u> without <u>breaking</u>. For example:

1) The rope in a tug-of-war resists <u>pulling</u> forces.
2) Bridge supports resist <u>squashing</u> forces.
3) A surfboard resists forces trying to <u>bend</u> it.

HARDNESS

1) This is the ability to withstand <u>scratching</u>, <u>rubbing</u> or <u>denting</u>.
2) Many <u>high-quality</u> graphic products need to be hard to avoid them getting scratched.

EXAM TIP
You get marks for <u>explaining why</u> a particular material is <u>suitable</u> for a product. E.g. 'because it's tough'.

TOUGHNESS

1) <u>Tough</u> is the <u>opposite</u> of brittle.
2) If a material is tough, it can <u>absorb impacts</u> without breaking or <u>snapping</u>.
3) <u>Armour</u> and bulletproof vests need to be tough.

IMPACT RESISTANCE

1) A sort of toughness, meaning the ability to withstand <u>a sudden force</u> without <u>cracking</u>.
2) Copper has good impact resistance — you can <u>hit it with a hammer</u> without it <u>shattering</u>.

FLEXIBILITY

1) Flexible materials can <u>bend</u> without breaking.
2) Electrical wires must be very flexible so they can <u>curve around</u> things.
3) Plastic rulers are quite flexible — they <u>bend</u> quite a bit before they break.

STRENGTH TO WEIGHT RATIO

1) Materials that are <u>strong</u> but <u>don't weigh much</u> have a <u>good</u> (high) strength to weight ratio.
2) This is important for things like <u>spacecraft</u> and <u>racing cars</u> that need to be <u>strong</u> but also <u>light enough</u> to go <u>really fast</u>.

Some live in bungalows, some in semi-detached...

Property jokes aside, you need to be able to say why a material is <u>suitable</u> for a product, and there's
only one way you can do that... you really need to get your head around what all these terms mean.

Properties of Graphic Materials

And last, but <u>definitely not</u> least:

AESTHETIC PROPERTIES

The way a material <u>looks</u> can be important when deciding what material to use.
1) <u>Opaque</u> means <u>light can't travel through it</u> (it's not see-through) e.g. a brick.
2) <u>Translucent</u> means <u>some light travels through it</u>, e.g. a thin, coloured acrylic sheet.
3) <u>Transparent</u> means <u>light travels easily through it</u> e.g. clear glass.
4) <u>Colour</u>, <u>texture</u>, <u>pattern</u> and how things <u>reflect light</u> can be important too.

Different Factors Affect your Selection of Material

If you understand the <u>properties</u> of all the available materials, you'll be able to pick the best one for the job.

PHYSICAL PROPERTIES

1) What <u>demands</u> will be made on the material?
   For example, it might have to hold <u>heavy loads</u>, be able to <u>bend</u>, or <u>protect</u> something from impacts.
2) Will it be used <u>outdoors</u> or <u>indoors</u>? For example, if it's going to be used outdoors you'll need to consider whether your material will <u>corrode</u>.

PRODUCTION METHOD

1) Some materials are easier to <u>join</u> than others. For example, <u>wood</u> can be glued, nailed, screwed...
2) The <u>material</u> must be suitable for the intended <u>production method</u> (and vice versa). For example, you can use <u>injection moulding</u> with plastics but certainly not with wood.

AESTHETICS

1) If the material is going to be seen, you want it to <u>look good</u>. For example, if it needs to fit in with a particular <u>environment</u>, it might need a certain <u>look</u>, e.g. <u>modern</u>, <u>traditional</u>.
2) Think about how the <u>finish</u> you apply (p. 30-31) will <u>change</u> the material's <u>appearance</u>. For example, painting wood will protect it, but it won't look rustic any more.

Practice Questions

1) Describe what is meant by the following <u>properties</u>:
   a) tough   b) opaque   c) flexible

2) Suggest a <u>product</u> that needs to:
   a) have good impact resistance   b) have a high strength to weight ratio

3) Suggest a <u>graphic product</u> for which <u>strength</u> is important, and say why.

4) Don is designing a <u>kite</u> that will be made by covering a frame. He is deciding whether to make the covering from paper, plastic or fabric.
   a) Suggest the <u>physical properties</u> that the <u>covering</u> material needs to have.
   b) Explain why Don should consider the <u>production method</u> before choosing a material.
   c) He reckons that the <u>aesthetic properties</u> of the material used for the <u>frame</u> are not very important. Is he right? Why?

Paper, Card and Board

There are lots of sorts of paper and board — each designed for a particular use. Paper and board are pretty useful for writing and sketching on (no, really) and also for making products like packaging.

You Need to Know About Four Sorts of Paper...

1) Cartridge paper has a textured surface, which is great for sketching with pencils, crayons, pastels, gouache, inks and watercolours.

2) Layout paper is thin and translucent (you can see light through it) and is used for general design work — particularly sketching ideas.

3) Bleed-proof paper is used by designers when drawing with felt-tips and marker pens. The ink doesn't spread out (bleed) — it stays put.

   Ink bleeds on some paper because the paper fibres suck the ink away.

4) Tracing paper is translucent, and is used to copy images.

...and Six Sorts of Board

The weight of paper and board is measured in gsm (grams per square metre). Above 200 gsm, it's not paper any more — it's board.

1) Solid white board has a high quality bleached surface, which is ideal for printing on. It's used loads for primary packaging.

   Primary packaging holds individual items. Secondary packaging is used to contain lots of primary-packaged goods.

2) Mount board is used to mount drawings and photographs for presentation or framing — usually by cutting a 'window' into the board.

3) Corrugated board is used a lot in secondary packaging to protect products during transit. See the next page for more on corrugated board.

4) Duplex board has a different colour and texture on each side. It's often used where only one surface is seen, so that only one side needs to be smooth for printing. It's unbleached, so it's ideal for food packaging.

5) Grey board is rigid. It's easy to cover with paper so that graphics can be displayed on it. It's found in game boards, hardback books, ring binders, and covered boxes.

6) Foam board is stiff but lightweight. It's used for mounting posters and making models.

I'm board — are we nearly there yet...

All these different types of paper and board are here for a reason — each one's best at a different job. Learn their properties in case you get asked which sort you should use in your exam paper... (Geddit?)

Paper, Card and Board

Corrugated Board is Strong For its Weight

1) <u>Corrugated</u> paper or board is made by sandwiching a wavy (fluted) <u>inner core</u> between <u>two outer layers</u>.

2) It's <u>strong</u> and able to <u>absorb impacts</u> (see p. 22), making it good for <u>packaging</u>.

3) The <u>air</u> in the gaps makes it a <u>good insulator</u> — so it's useful for wrapping takeaway <u>coffee cups</u>.

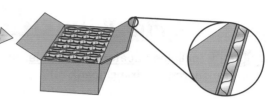

Another way to improve the properties of paper is by laminating it (see page 31).

You Can Buy Paper in Standard Sizes

1) Paper sizes go <u>from A0</u> (which has an area of 1 m²) to <u>A1</u>, <u>A2</u>, and so on — halving in size (area) each time.

2) Many other sizes are also available:
   - <u>A4</u> paper is <u>half</u> the size of <u>A3</u> paper.
   - <u>A5</u> paper is <u>half</u> the size of <u>A4</u> paper.
   - <u>A6</u> paper is <u>half</u> the size of <u>A5</u> paper.

   As the paper gets smaller the number increases.

   > The width of A3 paper is the length of A4.
   > The length of A3 paper is double the width of A4.

3) The most common paper sizes used in UK schools are <u>A4</u> and <u>A3</u>.
   A4 is 297 mm × 210 mm, in case you're interested.

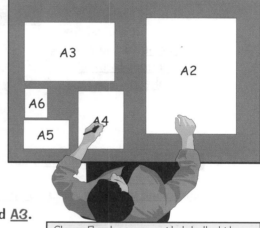

Clever Ben has correctly labelled these sheets of paper. Well done, Ben!

Practice Questions

1) What type of paper is often used for drawing with <u>felt-tip</u> and <u>marker pens</u>? Explain why.

2) a) What's the surface of <u>cartridge paper</u> like?
   b) What would you use it for?

3) What properties do <u>layout paper</u> and <u>tracing paper</u> have in common?

4) In what <u>units</u> are the weights of paper and card measured?

5) Describe <u>duplex board</u>, and say why it's used a lot in food packaging.

6) a) What's the difference between <u>primary</u> and <u>secondary</u> packaging?
   b) What type of board might you use for each?

7) Laura wants to make a sturdy ring-binder with pictures and text <u>printed</u> on the outside. What type of board would be best and why?

8) What <u>standard size</u> is this piece of yellow paper?

Plastic

There are two main types of plastic — thermosetting and thermoplastics. Luckily, you only need to know about <u>thermoplastics</u>. These are moulded by heating and can be <u>re-moulded</u> if you heat them again.

There are Many Different Thermoplastics

1) **Acetate** (<u>cellulose acetate</u>) is <u>flexible</u>, <u>hard</u>, <u>shiny</u> and <u>transparent</u> or <u>translucent</u>. It's used for packaging where the product needs to be <u>seen</u>. It's easy to print on. It's made mostly from wood so it's a bit more <u>sustainable</u> than many plastics.

2) **Polypropylene** (<u>PP</u>) is <u>quite strong</u>, <u>tough</u> and <u>flexible</u>. Products can be made with a '<u>living hinge</u>' (box, lid and hinge all made out of one piece of polypropylene) — which is handy for lunch boxes, etc. It's also used for <u>packaging</u>, <u>chairs</u>, <u>textiles</u> and <u>car parts</u>.

3) **High Impact Polystyrene** (<u>HIPS</u>) is rigid and comes in a variety of colours and thicknesses. It's used for making <u>boxes</u> for products and for <u>vacuum forming</u>. It's fairly <u>cheap</u>.

4) **Polyvinyl chloride** (<u>PVC</u>) is <u>cheap</u> and <u>durable</u>, easy to <u>print</u> on, but quite <u>brittle</u>. It's used for <u>blister packs</u> (e.g. for holding pills or screws), <u>vinyl records</u>, <u>insulation</u> for electrical wires, etc.

5) **Acrylic** is <u>stiff</u> and <u>durable</u> but it <u>scratches easily</u> and can be quite <u>brittle</u>. It <u>resists impact</u> well, so it's often used instead of glass, e.g. to make <u>aeroplane windows</u> and <u>aquariums</u>.

Plastics Can be Used for Modelling

The following plastic materials aren't very strong but they're <u>easy to cut and shape</u>. That makes them useful as <u>modelling materials</u> — for seeing your ideas in <u>3D</u>.

1) <u>Corrugated plastic sheet</u> or '<u>corriflute</u>' is <u>lightweight</u>, <u>rigid</u> and <u>weatherproof</u>. It's made from <u>polypropylene</u>. Although it's fairly stiff it can still be <u>bent into shapes</u>, so it's good for modelling objects with large <u>flat surfaces</u> and <u>square edges</u> — e.g. the outside cases of electronic items. It's also often used for estate agents' sign boards and students' folders.

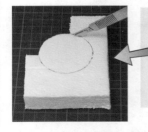

2) <u>Expanded polystyrene foam</u> is a <u>lightweight</u> material that you can shape with a <u>knife</u> or more accurately with a <u>hot-wire cutter</u>. Some types are quite <u>crumbly</u> (these types are often used as protective packaging). Other types have a fairly <u>dense structure</u>, e.g. **STYROFOAM**™ (which is usually <u>blue</u>). Expanded polystyrene foam is good for making 3D models.

The month before your exams — it's the vinyl countdown...

OK, so <u>revising plastics</u> is about as much fun as trainspotting while someone slaps you with a haddock. Still, it'll be <u>worth it</u> when you sit down in the exam and read a question that you can answer straight off.

Plastic

There are lots of different ways to <u>mould</u> and <u>shape</u> plastics. Here are a couple you need to know:

Air is Sucked Out In <u>Vacuum Forming</u>

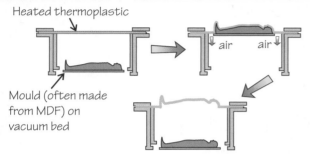

Heated thermoplastic

Mould (often made from MDF) on vacuum bed

1) A mould is put onto the <u>vacuum bed</u>.
2) A sheet of <u>thermoplastic</u> (e.g. **HIPS**) is clamped over the bed and is heated until it's <u>soft</u>. The bed is then lifted <u>close</u> to the heated plastic.
3) Air is <u>sucked</u> out from under the plastic, creating a <u>vacuum</u>. Air pressure from outside the mould forces the plastic onto the mould.

In vacuum forming, the moulds must have rounded corners and be slightly tapered (sloped) at the sides — so that the finished product can be released from the mould.

Strip Heating <u>Bends Plastic in a</u> <u>Straight Line</u>

You can <u>bend thermoplastic</u> with a <u>strip heater</u> or <u>line bender</u>. Here's how:

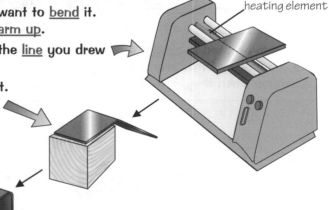

heating element

1) Draw a <u>line</u> on your <u>thermoplastic</u> where you want to <u>bend</u> it. Let the <u>element</u> (the hot wire) in the heater <u>warm up</u>.
2) <u>Hold</u> the plastic or rest it on the bars so that the <u>line</u> you drew is <u>over the element</u>, and <u>heat both sides</u>.
3) When the plastic has <u>softened</u> you can <u>bend</u> it. Bend it around a <u>jig</u> to get the <u>correct shape</u>, then leave it to cool and harden.
4) You can use this method to make things like <u>menu holders</u> and <u>table signs</u>.

Practice Questions

1) What does <u>PVC</u> stand for?
2) Steve wants to make <u>models</u> of his ideas for a new computer casing. Suggest a suitable <u>plastic</u> for modelling a design that has:
   a) square corners and flat sides?
   b) smooth, rounded corners and curved sides?
3) Rick has designed a card game. He's thinking about how best to <u>package</u> it. Suggest a suitable plastic if he wanted to sell the pack of cards:
   a) wrapped in a <u>see-through</u> plastic packet?
   b) mounted in a <u>card-backed</u> blister pack?
4) Describe the process of <u>vacuum forming</u>.
5) Emma needs to <u>fold</u> a piece of <u>acrylic</u> for the picture frame she is making.
   a) Name a process she could use to fold the acrylic.
   b) Outline what happens during this process.

Smart and Modern Materials

You can get special materials that can change in different conditions.

Smart Materials React to Their Environment

1) Smart materials change their properties in response to heat, light, or something else (depending on the material).

2) They often change back to their original state when the heat or light (or whatever else affects them) is taken away.

3) Some smart materials can let you make totally new products.

Smart Plastics Do All Sorts of Cool Stuff

1) Polycaprolactone (sometimes called a polymorph) is a type of plastic used for making models to try out new designs.

2) Its low melting point of 62 °C means that it can be made mouldable by immersing it in hot water. Polycaprolactone can be moulded and shaped by hand when warm, or machined when cold.

3) When fully cooled, it is stiff and strong (a bit like HIPS, see p. 26).

If you use polycaprolactone, don't overheat it, or you'll ruin it.

Smart Pigments Change in Response to Heat...

1) Thermochromic pigments change colour with heat (and go back to their original colour when they cool).

2) They can be used in paints to create images that change when they get hot, e.g. on mugs. Other products they're used on include oven dishes that warn you when they're really hot and feeding spoons for babies.

Blue spoon... ...gets hot... ...and becomes pink.

With her thermochromic spoon, Goldilocks was the terror of the local bear population.

3) Thermochromic inks also change colour reversibly in response to heat. They can be printed onto a substrate (e.g. plastic or paper), which can then be used for warning patches that tell you if something is too hot (e.g. on computer chips). They can be cheaper and more reliable than electronic heat warnings. Other uses include battery test panels and thermometers for fish tanks.

4) Thermochromic films are sheets that have been printed with thermochromic ink. You could use them for displays that change colour when touched, or when a hidden wire is heated by an electric current.

...Or Light

1) Photochromic pigments change colour reversibly in response to light.

2) They can be put into spectacle lenses to make glasses that turn into sunglasses when it's sunny.

3) Photochromic inks can be used to print t-shirts with designs that only show up in sunlight.

Supercalifragilisticpolycaprolactone...

If you've made a polymorph giraffe and got bored with it, just warm it up and make it into a gorilla. Shame there's no polymorph exams — "I'm fed up with French, think I'll do a bit of Art for a while."

Smart and Modern Materials

Phosphorescent and Fluorescent Pigments Are Bright

Phosphorescent pigments store light that hits them and slowly release it, so they glow in the dark. They're used for clocks and fun decorations, e.g. stars for bedroom ceilings.

Fluorescent pigments are really bright because they reflect lots of light.

As well as reflecting visible light, fluorescent pigments absorb UV light and reflect it as extra visible light — this is what makes them so bright.

They're used for safety signs and high-visibility jackets.

Nanomaterials Have Useful Properties

1) Nanotechnology involves really really really tiny particles (nanoparticles) — these are so tiny that you could fit about a thousand of them into the width of one of these hairs.

2) Nanoparticles include tiny crystals (nanocrystals) and tiny tubes (carbon nanotubes).

3) Nanotechnology has produced a wide range of clever 'nanostructured' materials because nanoparticles change the properties of the 'normal' material. E.g. nanostructured copper (made up of copper nanocrystals) is much harder and more rigid than ordinary copper (made of relatively large crystals).

4) Nanocomposites are made by combining nanoparticles with existing materials, e.g. composites of nanotubes and carbon-fibre are used to make bike frames and tennis rackets with high strength to weight ratios.

5) Here are some more examples of how they're used:
   - Nanoparticles are used to make anti-vandal paint (other paint won't stick on top).
   - Packaging materials can be made where the minute gaps in the product's structure are filled in with incredibly tiny bits of 'clay' (nanoclays). This makes them extra airtight, so food and drink last longer.

6) Some people are concerned about the safety of nanotechnology — it's so new that it's difficult to know what the risks are. They're worried that nanoparticles might react with body chemicals and cause harm, or cause damage to the environment.

Practice Questions

1) What is a smart material?

2) Give an example of what a smart plastic can be used for.

3) Paul is designing a can for his Dandelion and Burdock drink. He wants to make a label that will show when the drink is too warm. Suggest which type of smart material he could use for his label, and describe how it would work.

4) Describe briefly how glow in the dark stickers work.

5) a) What is a nanoparticle?
   b) Give two uses of nanomaterials.

Finishing

Special finishes can be used to make graphic products look fancier and last longer. Ooooh...

Laminating Means Sandwiching in Another Material

1) Laminating means <u>sandwiching</u> a document <u>between</u> two layers of something else — usually <u>plastic</u>. The laminating machine <u>heats</u> the plastic and <u>seals</u> it together. 'Laminating' is often used to describe covering <u>card</u> (or paper) with plastic.

2) Laminating <u>business cards</u>, <u>menus</u> and <u>posters</u> makes them last longer without getting <u>damaged</u>.

Embossing Leaves a Raised Impression

1) <u>Embossing</u> means pushing a <u>shaped die</u> into the back of the material to leave a slightly <u>raised impression</u> on its surface.

2) It's used to <u>draw attention</u> to a particular bit of the product, e.g. the <u>title</u> of a book, a <u>logo</u> or an <u>image</u>.

3) It's an <u>expensive</u> process but it adds <u>texture</u> and can suggest <u>quality</u>.

a quality Canadian number plate

Foil Application Makes Things Look Fancy

1) Foil application (or foil blocking) means using <u>heat</u> and <u>pressure</u> to <u>print metal foil</u> onto certain areas of a product.

2) Like embossing, it's used in packaging to <u>draw attention</u> to a <u>logo</u> or <u>brand name</u>, and to give the impression of a <u>quality</u> product — but it's <u>expensive</u>.

3) It's used on <u>expensive packaging</u>, <u>greetings cards</u> and <u>wrapping paper</u>.

Varnishing Makes Things Shiny and Hard-Wearing

Varnish is applied <u>after printing</u>, to give the impression of <u>quality</u> and provide <u>protection</u> against scuffs and scratches.

SPIRIT VARNISH is <u>cheap</u> but <u>slow-drying</u>.
It can be <u>gloss</u> (shiny), <u>matt</u> (dull) or <u>satin</u> (in between).
It's often used to cover a <u>whole piece</u> of paper or board to make it <u>shiny</u> and <u>hard-wearing</u>.

UV LACQUER <u>quickly</u> hardens when it's exposed to <u>ultraviolet</u> light.
It's really <u>shiny</u> and is often used to <u>spot-varnish</u> fancy book covers or chocolate boxes, to make <u>one bit stand out</u>.

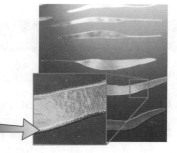

My mate stamped '0' on me — he liked embossing me round...

You might be able to use some of these <u>snazzy effects</u> in your graphics project, and make your ideas <u>stand out</u> from the dross that your friends have produced. But, of course, don't tell them I said that.

Finishing

Paper Can be Laminated to Improve its Properties

If you laminate paper or card by adding a layer of another material (it doesn't have to be plastic) you get a composite material with different qualities. For example...

> A composite material is one that's made up of two or more different materials.

Ernie misunderstood his boss's instruction to build a laminator.

POLYTHENE

Paper can be coated with polythene to make it waterproof.

Then you can use it for things like paper cups, where normal paper would go soggy pretty quickly.

POLYSTYRENE

Foam board is made by laminating polystyrene foam between card.

It's stiff but lightweight, and is used for mounting posters and making models.

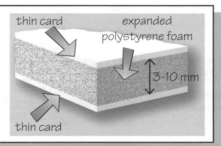

thin card

expanded polystyrene foam

3-10 mm

thin card

Second time round, the laminator was more successful — but still not quite right.

ALUMINIUM

Aluminium foil is added to food packaging (similar to foil application on previous page).

This keeps flavours in and air out — and you can print graphics onto the paper.

> Corrugated paper or board is a laminate too (see page 25).

Practice Questions

1) How can a product be improved by:
   a) laminating,   b) embossing,   c) foil application,   d) varnishing?

2) Cuthbert wants to make menus to stand on the tables of his new restaurant.
   Suggest a technique he could use to give the menus a professional-looking finish.

3) Describe the structure of foam board. Suggest what you'd use it for.

4) Delia has invented a new mustard, sherry and cheese sauce.
   She wants to package it in a paper carton.
   a) Suggest what material the paper should be laminated with.
   b) How would using this material change the properties of the carton?
   c) Suggest a possible environmental problem of using this composite material.

Joining Materials

There's an <u>adhesive</u> for almost <u>every</u> situation in life. Phew.

For Sticking Paper and Card

1) You use `glue sticks` to bond paper and card. They're <u>non-toxic</u>, <u>cheap</u> and come in different sizes. Common brands include Pritt®, UHU® and Bostik. They're all clear when dry and are <u>environmentally friendly</u>.

2) You can apply `rubber-based cement` (or <u>gum</u>) to <u>both surfaces</u> then leave for about ten minutes before bringing the surfaces together. <u>Repositioning</u> is possible.

3) The glue in squeezy `glue pens` is <u>liquid</u> — so it can be <u>messy</u> to use. Glue pens bond paper and card and the glue is <u>clear</u> when dry.

4) You can use `aerosols` such as <u>SprayMount</u>™ and <u>PhotoMount</u>™ for mounting photos onto paper or card — they cover large areas well and allow for <u>repositioning</u>.

For Sticking Wood Together

1) `Polyvinyl acetate (PVA)` glue is a <u>water-based</u> glue used to bond <u>wood</u>. It's also good for <u>paper</u> and <u>card</u> — though it takes a while to dry.

2) `Balsa cement` is good for sticking <u>balsa wood</u>. It's clear when dry.

3) You can use `glue guns` to quickly bond materials like <u>wood</u>, <u>fabric</u> and <u>card</u> together. They use a <u>low-melt plastic</u> that will <u>burn you</u> if it gets on your <u>skin</u>, so take <u>care</u>.

For Sticking Acrylic

`Acrylic cement` is also called <u>Tensol</u>®. It's used for <u>plastics</u> and is good for joints that won't be knocked.

For Sticking Most Materials

1) You need to mix the two parts (<u>resin</u> and <u>hardener</u>) of `epoxy resin` glue together — 'rapid' versions set in about 5 minutes, so speed is essential.

2) You get `superglue` in small tubes — it quickly bonds a large variety of materials, e.g. ceramics, plastics, textiles and metal (and your fingers).

Chad fell for the old epoxy resin/hair gel switch-e-roo

Knock-Knock — 'Who's there?' — 'U' — 'U who?'...

There are loads of <u>glues</u> to stick things together — with <u>more than one</u> for each type of material. Try to figure out which one <u>suits your needs</u> the best. Don't get stuck in a rut — there's a glue for you.

Joining Materials

Fixings Can Be Permanent...

1) <u>Double-sided sticky pads</u> can stick things together <u>quickly</u>...

2) ...and so can single and double-sided <u>adhesive tapes</u>.

3) <u>Clic (or plastic) rivets</u> are used to <u>join sheet material</u> (e.g. plastic) together. They're installed from <u>one side</u> — first you make a <u>hole</u> through the sheets then push the top of the rivet by hand.

4) <u>Press-fit 'click' fasteners</u> can also be used to join sheet material.

5) <u>Eyelets</u> are metal fixings used to <u>reinforce holes</u> in things like <u>banners</u>. <u>String</u> or ribbon can then go through the hole to <u>tie</u> the banner <u>up</u>. Eyelets can also be used to <u>join thin sheets</u> together e.g. in decorative cards.

PUSH

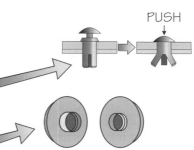

...Or Temporary

<u>Velcro®</u> <u>pads</u> are self-adhesive pieces of the <u>famous two-part hook and loop system</u>. They've got loads of uses — they're particularly good for displays.

Under a microscope the simplicity of Velcro® is easy to see.

<u>Press stud fastenings</u> are good for joining fabric bits together.

<u>Prong paper fasteners</u> join pieces of <u>paper</u> and <u>card</u> together as <u>movable joints</u>.

The fastener is inserted through a hole and then opened out.

Practice Questions

1) What type of <u>glue</u> would you use to stick:
a) two pieces of <u>paper</u> together?
b) <u>photos</u> onto a piece of <u>card</u>?
c) a piece of <u>paper</u> to a piece of <u>wood</u>?
d) your <u>hands</u> together?

2) Sally is using a <u>glue gun</u> to stick some fabric to a wooden frame. Give one <u>precaution</u> she should take.

3) Outline how <u>epoxy resin</u> is used.

4) Derek is making a model of a house using <u>cardboard</u>. He needs to fold his shape net up to form the 3D model, but he doesn't want to use glue. Suggest how Derek could <u>secure</u> his shape net without affecting the outside of the model.

Tools and Equipment

When you're making presentation drawings there are loads of different media to choose from.

Pencils are Ace

"You can lead a horse to water but a pencil must be lead." (Stan Laurel)

1) Pencils are made from a mixture of graphite (a form of carbon) and clay.

2) They are classified by their hardness (H) and blackness (B) and range from 9H (least graphite) to 9B (most graphite).

hardest   blackest

9H 8H 7H 6H 5H 4H 3H 2H H HB B 2B 3B 4B 5B 6B 7B 8B 9B

→ more graphite — softer

Harder pencils (e.g. 2H) are better for precise, technical drawing. HB is good for sketching.

3) Coloured pencils come in a variety of hardnesses — the softer ones produce an even, flat colour.

Inks, Paints, Pastels, Dry-Transfer Lettering... also Ace

INKS

These are pigments suspended in water or another solvent. They're good for colour infilling, background washes and writing.

CHALK PASTELS

You can use chalk pastel for backgrounds or to add tone and shading. It's easily blended using your fingers or cotton wool.

GOUACHE

Gouache is an opaque paint (not see-through). You can use it for flat areas of colour, or highlights on renderings (shaded drawings, see p. 39).

DRY-TRANSFER LETTERING

This is applied with pressure from a waxed translucent sheet onto drawings or 3D prototypes.

Airbrushes Blow a Mist of Ink

← air

1) Airbrushes blow a fine mist of ink from a reservoir using compressed air.

2) You have to mask all the areas you don't want to airbrush. Use low-tack clear film — and cut it with a craft knife so you get clean edges.

3) It's a good idea to wear a mask so you don't inhale the ink. Safety goggles will protect your eyes too.

Felt Pens and Markers Dry Quickly

1) Fine-liners come in a variety of thicknesses and colours. They're great for drawing fine, precise lines and outlining drawings, e.g. orthographic drawings.

2) Markers are available in hundreds of different colour tones. They're great for thicker lines. You can get markers with different tips (chisel, bullet and brush).

3) If you're using solvent-based markers, make sure you're in a well-ventilated place.

Let's draw this page to a close now — I'm in a brush...

Computer packages, e.g. Adobe® Photoshop®, can be used to create effects that look like they've been done by hand — they can produce graphics that look like they've been airbrushed or shaded with chalk.

Tools and Equipment

Drawing Boards can Make Drawing Easier

1) You can use a piece of blockboard or plywood as a basic drawing board.

2) Free-standing ones are more expensive and include a mechanism to adjust the angle of the board — and some have an integrated parallel motion or T-square for drawing horizontal and vertical lines.

Drawing Apparatus Increases Accuracy and Precision

Set Squares, Rulers and Protractors

1) Set squares are used for drawing and checking angles.

2) You use a 30-60-90° set square for isometric drawings (p. 55).

3) Either a 30-60-90° or 45-45-90° set square can be used for orthographic projections (p. 52).

4) Hopefully you know what rulers are for. Examiners hate wiggly lines that should be straight — so use a ruler.

5) Protractors are used to measure or draw angles.

EXAM TIP
Clean your set squares and ruler or you'll smudge things and the examiner won't be able to tell just how perfect your drawings are.

Curves and Templates

1) You can use French curves (or ship's curves) for drawing complex curves.

2) Flexicurves can be shaped into different profiles.

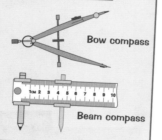

flexicurve

French curve template

3) You can use ellipse and circle templates to draw, errr, ellipses and circles.

4) Eraser guides protect a drawing while you're using an eraser. They make it easy to leave a highlight or tidy edge when erasing.

Compasses

1) You use these to draw arcs and circles.

2) Bow compasses are more accurate than those with an attached pencil.

3) Beam compasses are for larger drawings.

Bow compass

Beam compass

Practice Questions

1) Suggest what type of pencil you'd use for:
   a) sketching several initial design ideas,
   b) technical drawing.

2) Chris wants to add colour and shading to his design drawings. Suggest what equipment would be suitable for this, and explain why.

3) What piece of drawing apparatus would you use to draw:
   a) a 60° angle,   b) a circle,   c) a curve.

4) Use a protractor to draw an angle measuring 50°.

5) Use a pair of compasses to draw a circle with a diameter of 6 cm.

Cutting Tools

OK, you've probably known about scissors since you were old enough to run with them, but that's no excuse to skip these pages. There are plenty of other, more exotic cutting tools out there.

Good Old Scissors Cut Paper and Thin Card

1) You can cut paper and thin card well with scissors — but they're not much good for fine detail or for removing bits from within a sheet of paper or card (scalpels and knives are good for this — see below).

2) You can use 'pinking shears' to produce an interesting zigzag edge (which also helps stop fabric from fraying).

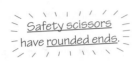
Safety scissors have rounded ends.

Craft Knives and Compass Cutters Cut Card and Paper

1) There are loads of different craft/trimming/hobby knives.

2) You mainly use these to cut card and paper — though some will cut thicker board, balsa wood, etc.

Surgical scalpels

These are very sharp and great for precision cutting.

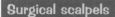

Metal cased knife

Stanley® knives, and other 'generic' types. These are good for tougher materials, e.g. thick board or balsa wood.

Circle cutters

You use these to cut arcs and circles in card and paper. You can vary the diameter of the arc or circle to be cut.

Plastic trimming knife

Similar to the metal cased knife, but some have retractable blades or blade covers for safety when not in use.

Perforation cutters

These have a round blade which rotates as you push it along, making a line of lots of small cuts. These can be used to make tear-strips, like the ones you find on forms where you're asked to detach a bit and send it back.

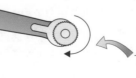
These are a bit like pizza cutters.

My Stanley just wasn't sharp any more — so he got the chop...

Take care when cutting — not only will you get a better cut, you won't get blood on your work.
Put all this equipment away safely too — don't just leave it at the bottom of your school bag. Ouch...

Cutting Tools

Safety Equipment _is Really Important_

When using cutting equipment, always take the right safety precautions.

When you're using a craft knife or any sharp cutting tool, it's best to use a cutting mat (to protect your work surface)...

...and a safety rule (to protect your fingers).

Guillotines **Cut** Large Sheets

1) You use guillotines to cut large sheets of paper and card, often many sheets at a time. They have a large blade that you push down.
2) Guillotines cut in a straight line to produce a nice straight edge.

Rotary cutters do the same thing, but they have a circular blade that gets pushed along.

Laser Cutters _are_ Expensive _but Can Make_ Detailed **Cuts**

1) Laser cutters are machines that cut out designs drawn using CAD. They can make really accurate and fine cuts through paper, card, plastic or wood. They can also be used to engrave things.
2) They use a very fine laser to burn away material — you'll need to use an extractor to get rid of fumes.

Die Cutters _and_ Creasing Bars **Cut** Shapes

A die cutter can be used to cut out nets to make packaging.

1) A die cutter presses out the net from the sheet of material, using a sharp blade specially shaped to the outline of the net — it's a bit like a pastry cutter.

2) Creases can be made (along the lines where the packaging will be folded) by rounded creasing bars.

3) You have to make blades especially to match your net, so die cutting is expensive to set up. But it's great for making large quantities of nets with complicated designs.

cutter   creasing
                           bar
          card

Practice Questions

1) What tool would you use to:
   a) remove a small shape from a piece of card?
   b) cut a circle from a piece of card?
   c) cut a piece of balsa wood?
   d) cut a magazine in half?

2) a) What can laser cutters do, other than cut through material?
   b) Give an example of a product that might be made using a die cutter.

3) Name two pieces of safety equipment you should use when cutting straight lines in a piece of balsa wood using a knife.

4) What safety precautions should you take when cutting MDF with a laser cutter?

Enhancement — Tone and Outlines

Enhancement techniques are all about making your drawings look <u>better</u> and more <u>realistic</u>. Realistic drawings help <u>clients</u> to understand a designer's ideas.

Colours Have Different Hues and Tones

1) <u>Hue</u> is just another word for <u>colour</u> — it's the <u>actual</u> colour (e.g. red, green, orange, etc.).

2) The <u>tone</u> of a colour (how <u>dark or light</u> it is) can be changed by adding <u>black or white</u> to it. For example, blue can have different tones, e.g. light blue, royal blue or navy blue.

more white

3) If you add more <u>white</u> to change the tone it's called a <u>tint</u>. If you add more <u>black</u> it's a <u>shade</u>.

4) Objects in the real world have <u>light</u> hitting them in different ways — this creates <u>different tones</u>.

For example, even if a shirt is only <u>one colour</u>, it will seem to have lots of <u>tones</u> when it's worn.

Adding details like this in your drawings will make them look <u>3D</u> and <u>realistic</u>.

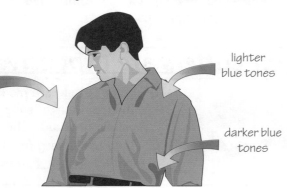

lighter blue tones

darker blue tones

You can also make your drawings look like they're made out of a <u>specific material</u> (e.g. wood) — see p. 41 for more info.

Pencil Shading Can be Used to Accentuate Shape

<u>Shading</u> can be added to a shape to make it look <u>3D</u>.

1) Shading a drawing to show <u>depth</u>, <u>light and shade</u> or <u>texture</u> is called <u>rendering</u>.

2) Different <u>pencils</u> can be used to create different <u>tones</u> — darker or lighter.

3) A <u>soft pencil</u> can create a wide <u>range of tones</u>.

4) Think about where the light's coming from — make areas <u>furthest</u> from the light the <u>darkest</u>.

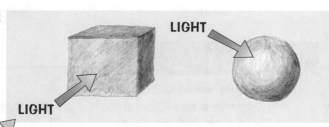

LIGHT

LIGHT

Keep out of the sun — do some shading...

You'll have to do fully rendered drawings in the <u>exam</u> as well as for your projects. Think carefully about what you're trying to show — there's more coming up on the next few pages about <u>texture</u> and <u>colour</u>.

Enhancement — Tone and Outlines

You Can Use a Pencil to Shade in Different Ways

There are several different shading techniques. Here are four common ones:

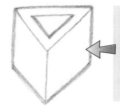

If you can see <u>both surfaces</u> that form a line, draw it <u>thin</u>. If you can only see <u>one surface</u>, draw a <u>thick line</u>. This gives the impression of solidity.

Use <u>highlights</u> to suggest a <u>reflective</u> surface. Add them by leaving <u>white</u> areas.

You can shade using <u>dots</u> — just use a <u>different concentration of dots</u> on each side. Some printers use this method, but it's fairly <u>time-consuming</u> by hand.

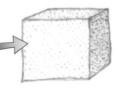

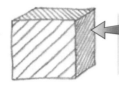

You can also shade using <u>lines</u>. You need to use <u>lines at different spacing</u> on each side. Lines at <u>different angles</u> can be used to show different colours, materials, etc.

You can show that an object has a really shiny surface by drawing <u>reflections</u> on it. This one's got a desert landscape on it.

Practice Questions

1) a) What is meant by the '<u>tone</u>' of a colour?
   b) How is the tone of a colour <u>changed</u>?

2) What's the difference between a tint and a shade?

3) What does <u>rendering</u> mean?

LIGHT

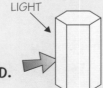

4) Copy the shape on the right.
   Use a <u>pencil</u> to shade it to make it look 3D.

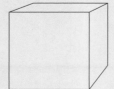

5) Copy the cube on the left.
   Use <u>thick and thin lines</u> to make it look solid.

6) What's the main disadvantage to <u>shading with dots</u>?

Enhancement — Texture

Giving your drawing <u>texture</u> will show what the object you've drawn is <u>made</u> of.

Draw the <u>Reflections</u> if <u>Metal</u> is <u>Shiny</u>

1) <u>Metals</u> can have a variety of colours and finishes.

2) You could have flat <u>sheet metal</u>, or metal with a <u>texture</u>.

3) <u>Textured metal</u> can be represented using <u>line techniques</u>, e.g. drawing lines to show any ridges, bumps etc.

4) When shading <u>shiny metal</u> look closely at what the <u>reflections</u> actually look like — and use <u>highlights</u> to show them.

5) <u>Chrome</u> is a really <u>shiny metal</u> which reflects things clearly and sharply. Add shading in the colours of the things it is reflecting.

6) There are no reflections on <u>matt metals</u>. Just pick out the <u>highlights</u>, which shouldn't be too sharp or bright — just use a lighter tone of the same colour.

EXAM TIP
Use some of the texture and tone enhancements from these pages to grab some extra marks.

There Are a Few Tricks for <u>Plastic</u>

1) <u>Marker pens</u> are useful for creating the look of <u>plastic</u>. Alternatively you could use <u>poster paints</u> or soft <u>coloured pencils</u>.

2) Plastic can have different <u>surface textures</u>. To show a <u>shiny surface</u>, make the edges <u>white</u> and keep the highlights <u>white and stripy</u>.

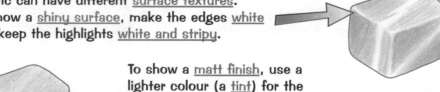

To show a <u>matt finish</u>, use a lighter colour (a <u>tint</u>) for the highlights (but not white).

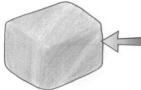

If it's textured plastic, show this by using <u>rough shading</u> to give the impression the surface is uneven.

3) <u>Pale</u> coloured <u>pens</u>, <u>paints</u> or <u>pencils</u> can be used to make an object appear <u>transparent</u>. You may even see other objects through the transparent object.

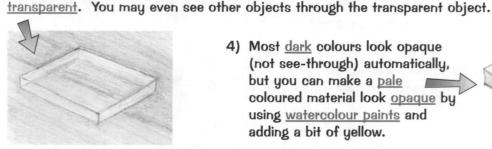

4) Most <u>dark</u> colours look opaque (not see-through) automatically, but you can make a <u>pale</u> coloured material look <u>opaque</u> by using <u>watercolour paints</u> and adding a bit of yellow.

So how do you make paper look like paper...

These techniques usually take a bit of <u>practice</u> — but this is GCSE Graphics, so they're pretty useful. Keep a sketch pad and colouring pencils with you, and if you find yourself with a spare five minutes...

Enhancement — Texture

You Can See What's Behind Glass

1) How you show glass depends on what's <u>behind it</u>. The glass itself is usually drawn with a <u>hint of blue</u>.

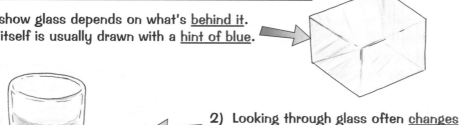

2) Looking through glass often <u>changes</u> the <u>lines</u> of the objects behind it — especially if the glass is <u>curved</u>.

Show Architectural Surfaces on Buildings

1) <u>Rough</u> surfaces like <u>concrete</u> and <u>cement</u> can be shown by putting <u>abrasive paper</u> underneath your drawing paper and shading with a colouring pencil. (Or you could always do it with lots of <u>little dots</u> — but this is very time consuming).

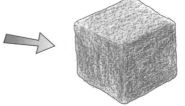

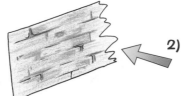

2) When you're showing <u>bricks</u>, you don't have to draw <u>every single brick</u> — that'd take ages — just pick out the <u>pattern</u> every now and then, and use different shades of <u>red</u> and <u>brown</u>.

For Wood, Use Colour and Draw a Grain

1) <u>Wood</u> can be drawn using <u>coloured pencils</u> to represent the <u>colour</u> and <u>grain</u>.

2) You can use more than one colour to get the <u>right shade</u>.

3) <u>Wood grain</u> can be added using a <u>darker</u> pencil. Remember that the <u>side</u> grain and the <u>end</u> grain look <u>different</u>.

Don't forget to draw the grain.

Practice Questions

1) What technique could you use to show the <u>reflections</u> in shiny metal?

2) a) Suggest two pieces of drawing equipment you could use to create the look of <u>plastic</u>.
   b) Suggest a way of making a pale coloured material look <u>opaque</u>.

3) Suggest what techniques and equipment you could use to draw <u>concrete</u>.

4) Suggest what techniques and equipment you'd use to draw a <u>block of wood</u>.

Enhancement — Colour

Picking the right colours can make your designs <u>stand out</u>.

Colours can make a Big Difference

1) The <u>right colour</u> can make a product look <u>more appealing</u> or create a <u>different mood</u>, or make it look more <u>expensive</u>, or more <u>fun</u>.

2) To <u>find</u> the <u>right colours</u>, you could try putting different colour <u>acetate</u> sheets over your drawing or have a look at <u>colour swatches</u> from paint shops.

3) Different <u>target groups</u> will often prefer different colours. Market research can help you to pick colours that your consumers will like.

Some Backgrounds Make Colours Stand Out

1) The way you <u>perceive</u> a colour can be affected by its <u>surroundings</u>.

2) The red stands out <u>vibrantly</u> against the black and white backgrounds. However, the red looks a bit <u>duller</u> against the orange and pink.

Colours Can be Used to Represent Mood

Colour is often used in graphic products to represent different <u>moods</u> or <u>feelings</u>.

To create a <u>heavy</u> mood, you might use a <u>dark solid colour</u>...

...while for a <u>lighter</u> mood you'd go for a <u>paler colour</u>.

Colours such as <u>red</u> and <u>orange</u> remind us of <u>fire</u> and the <u>sun</u> and so are known as <u>warm colours</u>...

...whereas <u>blues</u> are normally associated with <u>cold</u>.

Colours such as <u>blue</u> and <u>purple</u> remind us of <u>water</u> and the <u>sky</u> and are known as <u>cool colours</u> — these are generally quite calming colours.

Colours you find in <u>nature</u> such as <u>browns</u> and <u>greens</u> are known as <u>neutral colours</u>. They're also associated with <u>calm</u> or <u>relaxation</u>.

With all this green I feel so serene.

I only like the purple wine gums...

So if you're designing a leaflet to encourage people to stay at a friendly local **B&B** — don't make it angry stop-sign red. <u>Think</u> about what you want the colour to suggest, then <u>try out</u> a few ideas.

Enhancement — Colour

Some Colours Have *Particular Meanings*

<u>Red</u> often represents <u>anger</u> and <u>conflict</u> and can symbolise <u>danger</u>.

<u>Green</u> is a <u>calm</u> colour that is often used to represent <u>safety</u>.

EXAM TIP
Pick colours appropriate for your product — say why you've chosen them in your annotations.

Colours Can be *Organised into Different Groups*

There are two main groups of colours — <u>primary</u> and <u>secondary</u>.

1) The <u>primary colours</u> — red , blue and yellow — can be mixed together to produce many other colours.

2) <u>Secondary colours</u> — orange , purple and green — are colours made by <u>mixing</u> together primary colours. For example, <u>orange</u> is made by mixing together <u>yellow</u> and <u>red</u>.

3) Colour can be represented on a <u>colour wheel</u> which shows you how all the colours <u>fit together</u>. The <u>secondary colours</u> are made by mixing the primary colours on <u>either side</u> of them.

orange = red + yellow

purple = red + blue

green = yellow + blue

This colour wheel only applies to <u>paint</u> or <u>pigments</u> — not to <u>light</u>. (The primary colours for light are red, green and blue, which gives a different set of secondary colours too.)

Complementary *Colours Are Contrasting*

1) <u>Complementary</u> colours are found <u>opposite</u> each other on the <u>colour wheel</u> — green and red, purple and yellow, and orange and blue.

2) These colours are <u>contrasting</u> — they stand out against each other and can seem more <u>intense</u> together than when they're on their own.

In <u>CAD packages</u> you can <u>select</u> and <u>change</u> colours really easily. But if you're drawing by <u>hand</u> and you want to change the colours, you'll have to start your drawing again.

Practice Questions

1) a) How would you use colour to suggest a <u>lighter mood</u> in a product?
   b) List two <u>calming</u> colours.
   c) Why are road signs giving <u>warnings</u> coloured <u>red</u>?

2) Teddy wants to put a picture of a <u>red train</u> on a leaflet.
   a) What colour backgrounds would make the train <u>stand out</u>?
   b) What colour backgrounds would leave the red looking a <u>bit duller</u>?

3) a) What are the two main <u>groups</u> of colours?
   b) Name the three colours in each group.

4) Look at the colour wheel on the right.
   a) Which two colours should be mixed together to make <u>purple</u>?
   b) Which two colours should be mixed together to make <u>green</u>?

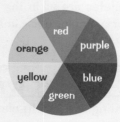

Colour Separation

Before we dive into colour separation, there are a few bits and pieces you should know first...

Colour Printers Use Four Colours in Layers

1) Colour printers use four colours — cyan, magenta, yellow and black (CMYK). These are known as process colours.

   The 'K' stands for 'key' — it means black. You can make black by mixing the other three colours, but using black ink usually looks better, and it works out cheaper if you're printing a lot of black.

2) Anything that's printed in colour is made up of a mixture of these colours.

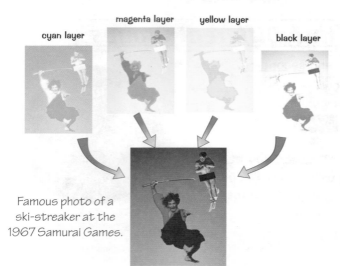

Famous photo of a ski-streaker at the 1967 Samurai Games.

3) When the computer is instructed to print, the printer recognises the required colour and adds layers of cyan, magenta, yellow and black to make the final colour.

4) Some printers use special spot colours (e.g. PANTONE® colours) as well — to print particular colours that can't be achieved with CMYK.

5) There's no set order in which the colours are put on to paper. Most printers stick to the CMYK order while others go from lightest to darkest — YMCK.

Commercial Printing Often Uses Printing Plates

1) Commercial printing is often done using lithography.
2) Lithography uses four aluminium printing plates — that's one plate for each of the CMYK colours.
3) The plates are coated in ink and used to press the image onto the printing surface.
4) The image is built up in layers of colour (as above).

Registration Marks Check the Position of the Plates

1) Printers use colour registration marks to check the printing plates are aligned in the right position.

2) If the printing plates aren't all in the right position, the image will be printed a bit fuzzy.

3) If the plates are all in the right places you get a single, clear image.

Black begins with a B — can't they spell...

Colour printing is a pretty clever thing. And it makes sense to mix four layers of colour, really — think how big printers would need to be if they had to contain cartridges of every single colour.

Colour Separation

Digital Printing is Good for Short Print Runs

1) Digital printing is used in <u>schools</u> and at <u>home</u> — <u>inkjet</u> and <u>LaserJet</u> printers are most commonly used. You can often get digital prints at high-street stationery stores or at the photo counters of supermarkets — just take a CD or USB memory stick.

2) You don't have to make <u>printing plates</u> like you do with traditional methods, so it's quick and every print can be different.

3) Because it's quick and cheap to set up, digital printing is often used to produce <u>proofs</u>. A proof is a first copy of the product sent to the client for approval in case changes are needed.

4) But it's expensive per sheet so commercial printers only use it for <u>short print runs</u> (up to about <u>3000 copies</u>). If more copies are needed then a more traditional method like <u>lithography</u> is cheaper.

Colour Separation, Well, Separates the Colours

If you've <u>hand-drawn</u> and coloured your design, you can print a full colour image of it. You just need to use a <u>digital scanner</u> to get it onto the computer. The scanner <u>separates</u> your drawing into different colours — red, green and blue:

1) The scanner uses <u>colour filters</u> which only let one colour through — either red, green or blue.

2) It takes <u>three pictures</u> of the image at the same time, each using a different colour filter.

3) Graphics software (or sometimes the printer itself) <u>converts</u> the RGB scan to <u>CMYK data</u> for printing. Instructions are sent to the <u>printer</u> about the CMYK colours needed for the image. The printer then prints the image by adding these four colours in layers.

4) If you've drawn your design using <u>CAD</u>, the printer can separate the colours — it has <u>colour separation software</u> built in.

Practice Questions

1) a) List the <u>four colours</u> that colour printers use.
   b) Outline how colour printers create <u>other colours</u>.
   c) Colour printers sometimes use '<u>spot colours</u>'. What are these used for?

2) What's this, and what is it used for? ⟶ ⊕

3) a) What type of printers are most commonly used for <u>digital printing</u>?
   b) Give <u>one advantage</u> of digital printing.
   c) Why might digital printing not be the best option for a print run of 10 000 copies?

4) Philippa has hand-drawn her design. She uses a <u>digital scanner</u> so that she can print out a full-colour image. What does the digital scanner do?

Presentation

Computer software is great for manipulating images quickly and painlessly.

Computer Pictures Come in Two Main Types

There are two types of image that are used on a computer — vector graphics and bitmaps.

1) Bitmaps are images made up of lots of tiny little bits called pixels. They're commonly saved as .jpeg, .bmp or .tiff. When they're increased in size they can go all blurry and pixelated (i.e. you see the individual pixels and not the picture).

2) Photographs are bitmap images. The higher the number of pixels the better, because the images will stay clearer when they're made bigger.

3) Vector graphics are images made of lines. They're commonly saved as .eps or .pdf. They can be made bigger or smaller without losing any quality. You can stretch and edit them by altering points on the lines.

4) Clip-art images are often vector graphics. Vector graphics also use less memory than bitmaps.

You Can Manipulate Images

1) There are lots of different programs you can use to edit images, e.g. Adobe® Photoshop® and CorelDRAW®.

2) You can alter your images by cropping (cutting bits off), resizing, rotating (turning around) and aligning them (lining objects up with each other).

3) More creative effects such as blurring, mirroring and distorting images can create cool designs.

centred   aligned left   aligned right

cat   mirrored   cropped   blurred   rotated   resized   distorted

4) Most image manipulation software can handle both bitmaps and vectors. The software will also let you add text to create things like posters and magazine designs.

Re-colouring is easy with vector graphics.

Most Images are Owned by Somebody

1) You can't just use any old image from the Internet in your own work — most of them will be copyright. This means that somebody owns the picture and you can't use it without their permission.

2) There are lots of image libraries on the internet. These contain thousands of images that you can buy to use in your work (sometimes they're free). A lot of design companies use these websites.

There may be restrictions on how you can use these images.

3) You can always take your own photo or design your own graphic instead...

Finding your way with pictures? Use a bitmap...

So, if you want a picture of the pyramids for some packaging, you could travel to Egypt to take your own photo and manipulate it to your heart's content. Or you could pay to use someone else's photo.

Presentation

Lettering Can Be Added to Products

1) Lettering varies from ornate, traditional styles to modern, dynamic styles.

2) Different lettering styles (fonts) are used for different purposes.

3) A traditional font, e.g. one with serifs or a script style wouldn't really be suitable for a trendy, up-to-date product.

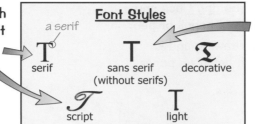

Font Styles

a serif

T serif

T sans serif (without serifs)

𝒯 decorative

𝒯 script

T light

4) In the same way, very modern fonts (these are mostly sans serif fonts) would look out of place on a product with a traditional, old-fashioned look.

5) Lettering that will be stuck on to a poster can be created by hand or using CAD.

6) Lettering designed using a CAD package can be sent to a CAM machine, e.g. a laser cutter, to be produced. This allows you to cut very accurate lettering from, say, sheets of acrylic.

Size and Alignment Can Make Text Easier to Read

There are lots of things you can do with text to make it more ergonomic (easier to read) or to make part of it stand out. For example, in this book important words are underlined and put in a different colour so they stand out better. Using bold, italic and different colours and fonts can also help.

1) Text needs to be big enough to read easily, but not so big that it looks silly or takes up too much room.

2) Font sizes are measured in points (pt). About 10-12 pt is good for text (this text is 11 pt). And 16-18 pt is good for headings (the heading above this text is 18 pt).

3) Alignment means how a block of text is arranged on the page.

Text can be aligned to the left. This is the most common way for normal text.

Text can be aligned to the right. This is used for some addresses on letters, and sometimes in magazines.

Centred text is sometimes used for titles or captions.

Justified text means that the edges of the text are all neat and level. It's used for blocks of text in things like fliers and newspapers.

Practice Questions

1) a) What are the two main types of image used on a computer?
   b) Which kind of image are photographs on computers?

2) Suggest two ways that photographs can be manipulated using computer software.

3) a) Why can't you take photos from a random website and use them on your product?
   b) What images can you use instead?

4) Say whether each of these fonts is serif or sans serif: a) Trout   b) Chump   c) Turnips

5) Jenny is designing a brochure for tourists visiting the ruins of an abbey. What type of font might she use? Explain your answer.

6) What type of CAM machine could be used to produce lettering for a plastic product?

7) a) Which alignment does this text have?   b) What is the name for this type of alignment?

Sketching

You <u>don't always</u> have to use <u>perfect</u> drawings. <u>Freehand sketches</u> are fine for getting across <u>initial ideas</u>. And they're pretty <u>easy</u> to do — so you can get <u>new thoughts</u> on paper <u>quickly</u>.

Freehand Sketching is Very Quick

1) <u>Freehand drawing</u> is where you <u>don't</u> use any <u>drawing equipment</u> apart from a pencil or pen.

2) It's the <u>quickest</u> method of drawing and is handy for getting <u>initial ideas</u> down on paper.

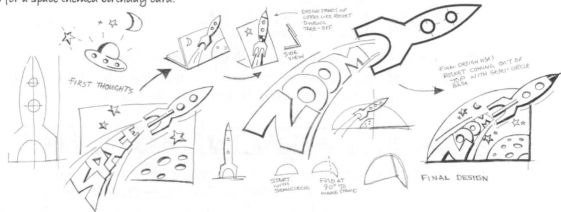

Ideas for a space themed birthday card.

3) You can <u>combine 2D</u> and <u>3D</u> sketches to show details.

4) And you can add <u>notes</u> to explain details, e.g. ideas for colours and materials.

5) <u>3D</u> freehand sketches often show how the <u>whole object</u> would look, while <u>2D</u> drawings tend to show the <u>details</u> of an object.

Start 2D Sketches with Rectangles and Squares

Standard <u>sketching</u> is very similar to <u>freehand</u> sketching, except that you start by <u>ruling guidelines</u>.

1) Using <u>vertical</u> and <u>horizontal</u> lines you can create squares and rectangles.

2) Use these to draw the <u>outline</u> of your shape first.

3) Details can be added by drawing more <u>squares</u> and <u>rectangles</u>.

4) Add <u>circles</u> and <u>ellipses</u> where necessary.

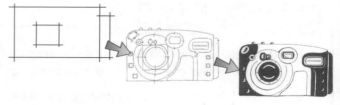

- Use <u>square boxes</u> to draw <u>circles</u> and <u>rectangular boxes</u> to draw <u>ellipses</u>.
- Mark <u>half way</u> along each side.
- <u>Join the points</u> to form the circle or ellipse.

If you've got a freehand, could you just help me with this...

And you thought sketching was just for doodling in the margins of your work... Make sure you get the hang of <u>crating</u> (see the next page). But don't do it for every sketch — freehand is much <u>quicker</u>.

Sketching

Draw More Accurately Using a Grid

1) You can lay grids under your page to improve the accuracy of your drawing.
(Or you could just draw on graph/grid paper.)

2) You could use an isometric grid, perspective grid or a square grid.

 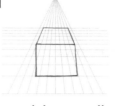

isometric   one-point perspective   square grid

Crating Can Be Used to Draw 3D Shapes

Crating is where you start by drawing a box — the 'crate' — and gradually add bits on and take bits off till you get the right shape. For example, you can remove sections from a cuboid to make any other 3D shape.

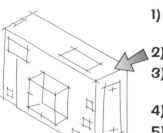

1) When you're sketching a 3D object, it's easier if you imagine it as a basic shape.

2) First draw the basic geometric shape faintly.

3) Stick to a particular drawing technique like two-point perspective or isometric (p. 54-55).

4) The object can then be drawn within the box.

5) Details of the object can be added by drawing more geometric shapes on top.

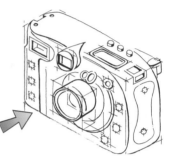

Crating Produces Wireframe Drawings

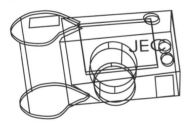

1) When you draw using the crating technique you can leave the solid sides of the shape unshaded.

2) Doing this lets you see straight through the object, as with this camera.

3) Wireframe can be used to show details on all faces of an object.

4) You can also view objects in wireframe in CAD software.

Practice Questions

1) a) What is freehand drawing?
   b) Suggest what you'd use it for.
   c) Why is it a good idea to annotate freehand sketches?

2) Draw an ellipse 40 mm wide and 70 mm long using guidelines.

3) a) Draw a cuboid with dimensions 30 mm × 30 mm × 40 mm using isometric paper.
   b) Suggest another type of grid that could be used for drawing in 3D.

4) a) What is crating?
   b) Draw a design for a radio using crating.
   c) What type of drawing does crating produce if the solid sides of the shape are left unshaded?

Basic Graphic Shapes

As well as sketching you have to be able to draw <u>accurately</u>, using a ruler and compasses and whatnot. These pages show you how to draw <u>basic shapes</u> — triangles, quadrilaterals, etc. So, sharpen that pencil...

There are <u>Different Types</u> of <u>Triangle</u>

All triangles have <u>three sides</u>. There are <u>four main types</u> of triangle:

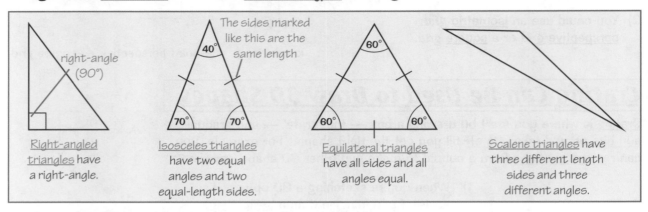

<u>Right-angled triangles</u> have a right-angle.

<u>Isosceles triangles</u> have two equal angles and two equal-length sides.

<u>Equilateral triangles</u> have all sides and all angles equal.

<u>Scalene triangles</u> have three different length sides and three different angles.

<u>Draw Triangles</u> <u>with a</u> <u>Ruler</u> <u>and</u> <u>Compasses</u>

You can use this method to draw a triangle with <u>any length sides</u>.

EXAMPLE:

Here's how to draw this triangle:

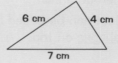

1 Draw <u>one of the sides</u> using a ruler. This gives you a base line.

7 cm

2 Set your compasses to the length of the <u>next side</u> (6 cm). Place the compass point at one end of the base line and draw a sweeping arc.

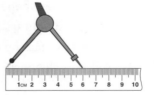

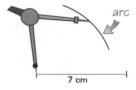

arc

7 cm

3 Set the compass to the size of the <u>final side</u> (4 cm) and draw a sweeping arc from the <u>other end</u> of the base line. The two arcs should <u>cross</u>.

7 cm

4 Join the <u>point where the arcs cross</u> to the ends of the base line.

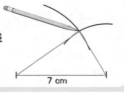

7 cm

<u>Nope — not an Indiana Jones type compass*...</u>

Once you've mastered these shapes you can <u>combine them</u> to draw all sorts of objects. Of course, CAD makes it a doddle to draw basic shapes but you need to know the old fashioned way too.

Basic Graphic Shapes

Learn These Quadrilaterals

A <u>quadrilateral</u> is any flat, <u>four-sided</u> shape. Here are some special ones...

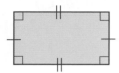

<u>Rectangle</u>

<u>Square</u>

<u>Rhombus</u>

<u>Parallelogram</u>

<u>Trapezium</u>
(one pair of
parallel sides)

<u>Trapezoid</u>
(no parallel sides)

Regular Polygons _Have All Sides The_ Same Length

You need to know these
<u>regular polygons</u> ➡

<u>Regular
pentagon</u>
(5 sides)

<u>Regular
hexagon</u>
(6 sides)

<u>Regular
octagon</u>
(8 sides)

Here's one way of drawing <u>any regular polygon</u>:

1. Start with a <u>circle</u> the size you want your shape to be and mark the centre.
2. There are <u>360°</u> in a circle. Divide this by the <u>number of sides</u>. For a pentagon, <u>360° ÷ 5 = 72°</u>
3. Split the circle into sectors of this size with a <u>protractor</u>.
4. <u>Join</u> the points on the circle to make the shape.

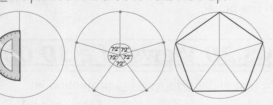

Hexagons are special. You can draw them this way.

1. Start with a <u>circle</u> the size you want your hexagon to be.
2. Keep your compasses set at the <u>same size</u> and draw <u>arcs</u> around the edge of the circle.
3. <u>Join</u> the points on the circle to make the <u>hexagon</u>.

Ellipses _are_ Stretched Out Circles

1) Ellipses are made from a continuous, smooth <u>curve</u>.
2) You can use an <u>ellipse template</u> to draw them, or you can sketch them using <u>circles</u> or <u>rectangles</u> to guide you.

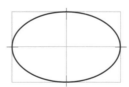

Mark half way along each side
of the rectangle. Join the
points to form the ellipse.

Practice Questions

1) Name <u>four</u> different types of triangle and <u>sketch</u> an example of each type.

2) Accurately draw a triangle with three sides of <u>6 cm</u>. What type of triangle is this?

3) What is a <u>quadrilateral</u>?

4) Construct a <u>regular octagon</u>.

5) Construct a <u>regular hexagon</u> using just a pair of compasses, a pencil and a ruler.

Working Drawings

Once you've <u>perfected</u> your <u>design idea</u>, you'll need to produce an <u>accurate working drawing</u> so that the manufacturer can make it. So guess what's coming up on these pages...

Scale Drawings are Used to Draw Big Things (but smaller)

1) To draw a <u>big object</u> on a small piece of paper, you have to <u>scale it down</u>.
2) The object's still drawn in <u>proportion</u> — it's just <u>smaller</u>.
3) The <u>scale</u> is shown as a <u>ratio</u>. For example:

> - A scale of <u>1:2</u> means that the <u>drawing</u> is <u>half the size</u> of the <u>real object</u>.
> - A scale of <u>1:4</u> means that the drawing is <u>a quarter of the size</u> of the real object.
> - Anything drawn at <u>1:1</u> is <u>full sized</u>.

4) The <u>scale</u> needs to be <u>clearly</u> shown on the diagram. It's a ratio, so it <u>doesn't have any units</u>.

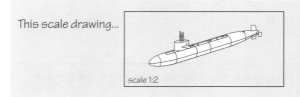

This scale drawing...

scale 1:2

... is half the size of this toy submarine.

5) To <u>check</u> you've scaled an object down properly, <u>measure</u> the lengths of the lines in your <u>drawing</u>. If you <u>multiply</u> those lengths <u>by the scale</u>, you should get the dimensions of the <u>real object</u>.

6) Lines on a scale drawing should be labelled with the <u>lengths</u> of the <u>real object</u> — <u>not</u> the lengths of the lines on the paper.

You can also scale things up. A scale of 2:1 means the drawing is twice the size of the real object.

Orthographic Projection Shows 2D Views of a 3D Object

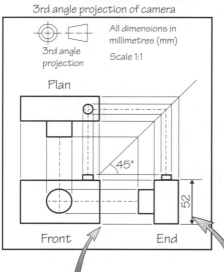

3rd angle projection of camera

3rd angle projection

All dimensions in millimetres (mm)

Scale 1:1

Plan

45°

52

Front   End

34

There's always a <u>gap</u> between the <u>projection lines</u> and the <u>object</u>.

1) The <u>symbol</u> for <u>3rd angle orthographic</u> projection is:
2) The <u>front view</u>, <u>plan view</u> and <u>end view</u> of the product are drawn <u>accurately to scale</u>.

> To draw an orthographic projection, you draw the <u>front view</u>, then:
> 1) Add construction lines going <u>up</u> to draw the <u>plan view</u>.
> 2) Add construction lines to the <u>right</u> to draw the <u>end view</u>.
> 3) Add the <u>dimensions</u> — these must always be in <u>millimetres</u>.
> Using <u>square grids</u> makes these drawings much easier.

3) To avoid confusion, lines and dimensions must conform to the following <u>British Standards</u> recommendations:

<u>outlines</u>: thick and continuous
<u>construction lines</u>: light and continuous
<u>centre lines</u>: alternate short and long dashes, light
<u>hidden details</u> (e.g. edges you can't see): short dashes, light
<u>dimension lines</u>: medium and continuous, with solid arrowheads and the dimension written above the line in the middle (or to the left of the line if it's angled or vertical)

Working drawings — even graphics have to earn a living...

Working drawings are all about <u>conveying information</u> — usually between the <u>designer</u> and the person <u>making</u> the product. That information has <u>got to be accurate</u> — or the product won't get made right.

Working Drawings

Assembly Drawings Show How Parts Join Together

There are a few different types of <u>assembly drawing</u>:

Fitted assembly drawings show the parts already fitted together. They can be in <u>2D or 3D</u>.

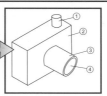

Exploded views are much more exciting — they're always in 3D.

- <u>Each separate part</u> is <u>moved out</u> as if it's been exploded.
- Each part is <u>drawn in line</u> with the part it's attached to — dotted lines show where the part has been <u>exploded from</u>.

You often get a <u>parts list</u> with an assembly drawing.

Item number	Part	Quantity
1	shutter release	1
2	camera body	1

Sectional Drawings Show Internal Details

1) Sectional drawings show what the product would look like inside if you <u>cut it in two</u>.

2) A <u>front view</u> of the object shows <u>where</u> the 'cut' has been made.
   In this diagram of a camera it's been cut through section XY.

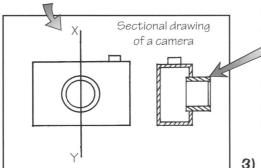

Sectional drawing of a camera

- <u>Cross-hatched lines</u> are used to show where the product has been 'cut'.
- The hatching is normally drawn at a <u>45° angle</u> with the lines <u>evenly</u> spaced.
- <u>Different parts</u> are hatched in a <u>different way</u>. In this diagram the lines are running in <u>opposite directions</u>.

3) Sometimes more than one section is shown, so each section line must be <u>labelled</u> very clearly.

Practice Questions

1) a) What does this mean?

scale 1:4

? mm

b) What is this measurement in real life?

2) When you're adding <u>dimensions</u> to a drawing, what <u>units</u> should they be in?

3) a) Suggest a type of drawing that is suitable for <u>self-assembly</u> instructions.
   b) Explain why this type of drawing is suitable.

4) a) What kind of drawing shows you the <u>front view</u>, <u>plan view</u> and <u>end view</u> of an object?
   b) The diagram on the right shows the front and plan views of a toaster. Complete the diagram to show the <u>end view</u>.

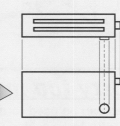

Section 4 — Types of Drawings

Pictorial Drawings

Pictorial drawing is just a fancy way of saying 'drawing in 3D'. You can really show off your design ideas with these techniques — flippin' useful stuff if you ask me.

Perspective Drawing Uses Vanishing Points

1) Perspective drawing tries to show what something actually looks like — smaller in the distance, larger close to. It does this by using lines that appear to meet at points called vanishing points.

2) These points are in the distance on the horizon line.

3) Perspective drawing is great for producing 3D drawings of products, packaging and point-of-sale displays (eye-catching sales promotions you find near check-out counters).

Use One-Point Perspective to Draw Objects Head On

1) One-point perspective only uses one vanishing point.

2) For example, here's how to draw a cube using one-point perspective.

  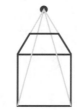

1) Mark one vanishing point.

2) Draw the front view of the object head on.

3) Then draw lines connecting the corners to the vanishing point.

4) Use these lines to complete the 3D shape. Hey presto.

3) You could use the same four steps to draw any object in one-point perspective.

Use Two-Point Perspective to Draw Objects at an Angle

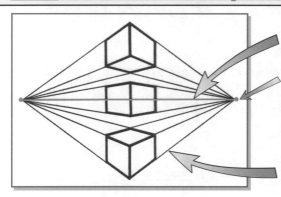

Two-point perspective shows objects edge-on.

1) Draw a horizon line horizontally across the page.

2) Mark two vanishing points — one at each end of the horizon line.

3) Draw the object by starting with the front, vertical edge and then projecting lines to the vanishing points.

4) Remember that vertical lines remain vertical and all horizontal lines go to one of the vanishing points.

5) The object appears different depending on whether it's drawn above, below or on the horizon line.

Don't worry too much — keep it in perspective...

These techniques can be used to draw all sorts of things, but the only way to get good at using them is to practise. To make your drawings even more realistic, try out the shading techniques in Section 3.

Pictorial Drawings

Isometric Drawing *Shows Objects at 30°*

1) Isometric drawing can be used to show an object in <u>3D</u>.

2) It <u>doesn't show perspective</u> (things don't get smaller in the distance), but it's <u>easier to get dimensions</u> right than in perspective drawing.

3) Isometric drawing shows <u>three sides</u> of the object. It's useful for drawing <u>products</u> and their <u>packaging</u>.

4) There are <u>three main rules</u> when doing isometric drawings:

> • Vertical edges are drawn as vertical lines.
> • Horizontal edges are drawn at 30°.
> • Parallel edges appear as parallel lines.

This drawing's been done on isometric <u>grid paper</u>.
You could use plain paper and a <u>30°-60°-90° set square</u> instead.

You can also draw more <u>complicated</u> shapes, e.g. <u>circles</u>.

   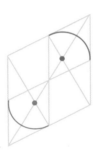 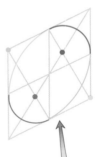

Start off by drawing an <u>isometric crate</u> — a 'square' skewed by 30°. (Draw it faintly — it's only a guide.)

Divide the crate up <u>horizontally</u>, <u>vertically</u> and through the <u>long diagonal</u>.

Now it gets trickier. Join the <u>two corners</u> on the short diagonal to the <u>mid-points</u> as shown.

Place your compass point on the <u>blue dot</u> and draw the <u>blue arc</u> shown. Repeat with the green dot.

<u>Complete</u> the isometric circle by placing your compass point in the <u>corners</u> marked and drawing the <u>arcs</u> shown.

Practice Questions

1) Name two <u>3D</u> drawing techniques.

2) What is a <u>vanishing point</u>?

3) A company wants you to design a point-of-sale display for their new chocolate bar.
   a) Sketch the outline of a chocolate bar using <u>one-point perspective</u>.
   b) Now draw it <u>above</u> the horizon line using <u>two-point perspective</u>.

4) Bob is doing an isometric drawing.
   At what <u>angle</u> should he draw the horizontal edges of the object?

5) Fred wants to advertise his new board game with a picture of a dice.
   a) What kind of drawing should he use to show <u>three sides</u> of the dice with the <u>right dimensions</u>?
   b) Draw a <u>dice</u> using the technique named in part a).

Nets and Packaging

Everything you ever wanted to know about <u>surfaces</u>. Apart from the surface of the moon.

3D Objects **Can be Made from** 2D Nets

A <u>net</u> is a <u>2D</u> plan for making a <u>3D</u> object. Nets are also called <u>surface developments</u>. You need to be able to <u>draw a net</u>...

Just remember to think about:

- how many <u>sides</u> the object has
- what <u>size</u> and <u>shape</u> each of these sides is
- how it all <u>fits together</u>

It might help to <u>imagine unfolding</u> your object.

Cube

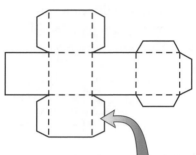

When drawing a net, use:

- <u>solid lines</u> to show which edges you're supposed to <u>cut</u>
- <u>dotted</u> or <u>dashed lines</u> to show which edges to <u>fold</u>

Don't forget to include <u>tabs</u> in the design of your net — so that you can <u>stick</u> it together at the end _(there's more about tabs on the next page)._

Here are some more <u>lovely nets</u> that you need to be able to draw:

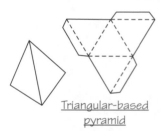

Triangular-based pyramid

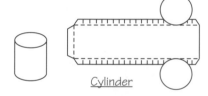

Cylinder

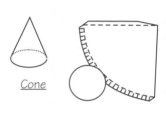

Cone

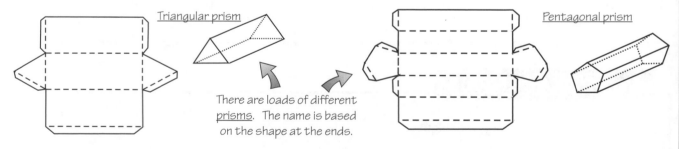

Triangular prism

There are loads of different <u>prisms</u>. The name is based on the shape at the ends.

Pentagonal prism

Nets are Useful for Modelling **and** Packaging

1) Nets are great for <u>modelling ideas</u>. You draw the net onto a <u>flat sheet</u> of material (e.g. paper, card, acrylic) and then <u>cut</u> it out and <u>fold</u> it into the 3D shape.

2) In <u>industry</u>, the net would be designed with <u>CAD</u> and cut out using <u>CAM</u> (see pages 70-71). It'd then be <u>folded</u> and <u>glued</u> together.

3) <u>Flat-packed packaging</u> is made from nets. It's a really useful type of packaging as it doesn't take up much space, making it <u>easy to store</u> and <u>transport</u> in large quantities.

Net yourself some marks — do a surface development...

As well as being great for making <u>models</u> and <u>packaging</u>, nets are also used to make flat-packed products like <u>point of sale displays</u>. They're easy to transport around and are dead quick to <u>assemble</u>.

Nets and Packaging

Flaps and Tabs Hold Things Together

After you've folded your 2D net into your 3D shape, you need to <u>hold it together</u> somehow.
There are different <u>fixing methods</u> — it depends what you're trying to do.

GLUE TABS

By applying <u>glue</u> to the <u>tabs</u> shown around the nets on the previous page, you can make <u>strong</u>
<u>permanent</u> joints. This type of joint is often found down the <u>side</u> or <u>base</u> of a package.

FOLD-IN FLAPS

These are great when a package needs to be opened and closed <u>more than once</u>.
They're found on loads of <u>box lids</u> — no glue is involved.

CGP
TEA BAGS
Ideal for revision

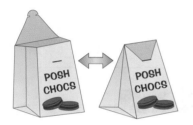

POSH CHOCS

POSH CHOCS

SLOT AND TAB MECHANISMS

You can open and close these
over and over again too.
They're <u>more secure</u> than fold-in flaps.

The card needs to be
quite <u>thin</u> for this
fixing method to work.

CRASH-LOCK BASES

These are used at the <u>bottom</u> of containers.
The container can be <u>flattened</u> for storage or
transport — then when it's needed the <u>base</u> is
<u>pushed out</u> to make a secure structure.

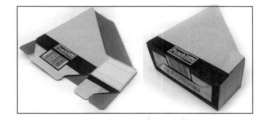

Practice Questions

EXAM TIP
You might be asked about
'developments' — don't forget
that these are just nets.

1) Describe how nets can be useful in the <u>design</u> process.

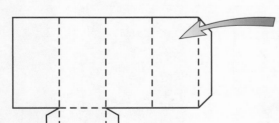

2) a) Draw the 3D object made from this net.
   b) What do the <u>solid lines</u> mean?
   c) What do the <u>dashed lines</u> mean?

3) Imagine you're eating a Toblerone®. Mmmm.
   Now draw a <u>net</u> of its packaging.

4) Draw an accurate net for a <u>hexagonal prism</u>.

5) Suggest which <u>fixing methods</u> would be good to use in a
   box to hold gerbils on their way home from the pet shop.

Charts and Graphs

Graphs and charts can show information so that it's easy to understand. It's really important to pick the type of chart that shows your data most effectively, rather than the one that you think'll look prettiest.

Bar Charts Use Bars to Show Numbers

EXAM TIP
Always give a graph or chart a title, and don't forget to label the axes.

1) A bar chart should have equally spaced bars of the same width.

2) The bars can be drawn horizontally or vertically.

3) It's easy to compare results using a bar chart — this one shows that more people like pictographs best than like bar charts or pie charts best.

4) Data can also be displayed in 3D bar charts. They're just the same, except the bars look solid.

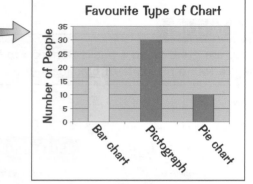

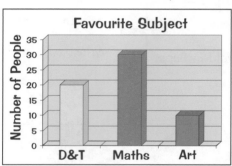

ICT is brill for drawing graphs

If you put the data from your market research into a spreadsheet, you can get the computer to draw a chart or graph.

It'll be really neat — plus you can update it quickly if necessary (if you manage to collect some more data, say).

Pictographs are Charts Made of Pictures

1) Pictographs (aka pictograms) use symbols or simple pictures — they can make slightly dull information look a little bit more interesting.

Average Hours of Sunshine a Day for Different Months

Month	Average Hours of Sunshine
October	☀ ☀ ☀ ☼
November	☀ ☀ ☼
December	☀ ☼
January	☀ ☀ ☀
February	☀ ☀ ☼
March	☀ ☀ ☀ ☀ ☼

☀ represents 2 hours of sunshine per day

So half a sun symbol means 1 hour of sunshine per day.

2) They must have a key to show what the symbol means.

This week's Top 40 Charts — at number 40, Pie...

They say you're never more than 3 metres from a maths question. Still, at least this lot isn't too bad. And it's more than half a pie likely to come up in the exam — so you'd better get on and learn it well.

Charts and Graphs

Pie Charts **Show** Proportions

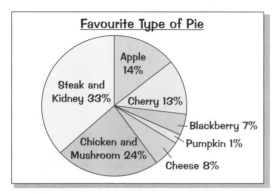

Favourite Type of Pie

1) Pie charts make it really easy to <u>compare</u> the sizes of different categories.

2) You might want to show the <u>percentage</u> for each category. (Check that the whole pie adds up to 100%.)

3) You can also draw pie charts in <u>3D</u>.

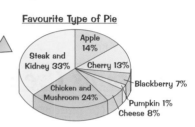

Favourite Type of Pie

Line Graphs **are for** Continuous Data, **like** Time

1) Line graphs show the <u>relationship</u> between <u>two factors</u>, e.g. speed and time.

2) You <u>plot</u> the information on the graph and draw a <u>line</u> through the points.

3) These are pretty handy for <u>spotting trends over time</u>, and also for spotting "<u>blips</u>".

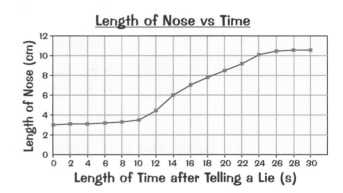

Length of Nose vs Time

Practice Questions

1) What's the main difference between a <u>bar chart</u> and a <u>pictograph</u>?

2) What <u>percentage</u> does a full pie add up to when you draw a pie chart?

3) 25 examiners were asked to name their favourite hobby — here are the results:

Favourite Hobby	Number of Examiners
Writing questions	12
Swotting up	9
Giving marks	3
Sleeping	1

a) Plot it all in a lovely <u>bar chart</u>.
b) Now show the information in a <u>pictograph</u>.
c) And why not put it in a <u>pie chart</u> too?
d) Which of your graphs and charts do you think shows the data the <u>best</u>? Explain your answer.
e) Why isn't a <u>line graph</u> a suitable graph for this data?

4) Draw a line graph to show this data:

Month	Jan	Feb	Mar	Apr	May	Jun	Jul	Aug	Sep	Oct	Nov	Dec
Birds counted in my yard	2	1	3	6	10	14	15	15	13	9	5	2

Signs and Labels

"A picture's worth a thousand words", or so they say. Some pictures are worth exam marks too.

Iconic Labels are Simple and Easily Recognised

1) Examples of iconic labels (or icons) appear on your computer screen as shortcuts to software, files or program tools.

2) Icons that identify functions (e.g. the text tool or the print symbol) are similar in all software packages, to help a user to quickly learn how to use new software.

3) Icons are usually small, and immediately recognisable to the user.

Make sure you know the main icons used in software packages, like the print symbol.

Ideograms Use Pictures to Represent Objects and Ideas

1) Ideograms (or pictograms) can be substituted for writing — they're kind of a universal language.

2) You'll have seen plenty of ideograms in everyday life — e.g. you might see a sign with an aeroplane to identify an airport, or one with a telephone receiver pointing to a payphone.

3) Ideograms sometimes show how to operate a product. For example, the control buttons on a stereo are pretty much universally recognised.

4) This recycling symbol means that some (or all) of the product can be recycled (see p. 67).

EXAM TIP
You might get asked to design a symbol or ideogram in your exam.

Ideograms Can be Created for Any Object

If an ideogram doesn't already exist for an object, you can create one — just follow these rules.

1) Simplify the object — just show the main features.
2) Don't use any words, then it can be used in any country.
3) Make sure it's an appropriate colour.

There are some standard colour conventions worth remembering:
1) Red for STOP or warning
2) Green for GO or OK or for something environmentally friendly or vegetarian

Labels Can Give Product Information

1) There might be information about how to store or maintain the product, or specific safety warnings.

2) Many products carry symbols that have an agreed meaning throughout Europe. For example, this 'e' means that the average bottle from the batch contains at least 100 ml of lotion.

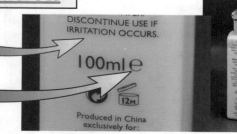

DISCONTINUE USE IF IRRITATION OCCURS.

100ml e

12M

Produced in China exclusively for:

Take it as a sign — you need to get this lot learnt...

There's a fair old bit to learn here, but you do need to know it. When you're designing a sign or label of your own, the most important thing is to make it really, really clear and dead easy to understand.

Signs and Labels

Products are Labelled if they Meet Certain Standards...

1) There are various organisations that set standards for certain types of product. These standards are usually about safety and the quality of design.
2) Products that meet these standards can usually be labelled to show this.
3) If a company's products meet these standards they might be more profitable — many consumers are more willing to buy 'approved' products, or will pay more for them.

The British Standards Institution (BSI) is one example of a standard writing organisation. The BSI independently tests products to make sure they meet British, European or International standards. For certain products (such as glass, windows or plastic pipes) a Kitemark can be awarded.

Certain types of product must also meet EU standards for safety, shown by the 'CE' mark, before they can be sold in most European countries.

The International Organisation for Standardisation (ISO) also issues certificates to organisations that meet international standards of quality. The label ISO 9000 shows that a product is quality assured.

...And To Show That You Can't Steal an Idea

The © symbol shows copyright

This shows that something is protected by copyright law and mustn't be copied. It appears on written or recorded work like song lyrics, software, drawings and art work. If someone wants to reproduce the work, they need to get the permission of the person who owns the copyright.

Trademarks are shown by a ™ mark

Trademarks are the symbols, logos, words or slogans that are used to represent companies, e.g. Google™ — other companies can't copy them.

Registered trademarks are shown by an ®, e.g. Microsoft®. (Even colours can be trademarks, e.g. the particular turquoise on tins of Heinz baked beans is a trademark.)

Practice Questions

1) What do you call pictures that are used to represent objects and ideas?
2) Jonny has just bought a new stereo.
   a) Draw the ideogram that might be on the "pause" button.
   b) Design an ideogram that tells the user to keep the stereo out of direct sunlight.
3) What would 400 g ℮ mean on a tin of tuna?
4) a) What is the name of the symbol on the left?
   b) What does it mean if a product is labelled with this symbol?
5) What does the 'CE' mark show?
6) What does © mean?

The 6Rs

This section is all about making your products more environmentally friendly — and keeping the 6 Rs in mind when you're designing is one of the best ways to do it.

Avoid Unnecessary Waste with the 6 Rs

All products have an impact on the environment at every stage of their life cycle — from the processing of raw materials, to manufacture, product use and disposal.

Trees are cut down... ...and made into paper... ...which is used to make notepads... ...which are then disposed of

REUSE

1) Customers can extend a product's life by using it again, e.g. refillable printer cartridges.

2) Some people reuse products for other purposes, e.g. using an old table as a workbench.

3) Reusing a product means you don't have to use up more material making a replacement.

RECYCLE

1) Recycling means reprocessing material rather than just re-using a product. It usually uses less energy than obtaining new materials.

2) Loads of stuff can be recycled, including paper, card, glass, aluminium and some plastics. Recycled card and plastic are often used to make packaging. Recycled paper is often used in newspapers.

Primary recycling is making the same thing.

e.g. a drinks can...

...gets melted down and made into ...

...another drinks can

Secondary recycling is making a different thing.

e.g. a HDPE drinks bottle...

...gets melted down and made into...

...a HDPE toy

Tertiary recycling is breaking something down to its raw materials.

e.g. a PET drinks bottle...

...is broken down chemically...

...and used as fuel to make more plastic.

3) Disassembly is also part of recycling. Some products, like cars, can be taken to pieces and the parts can either be recycled to make new products or used to repair other cars.

REFUSE

1) You can refuse to buy a product if you think it's wasteful — e.g. it might use a lot of unnecessary packaging or need a lot of energy to run.

2) When you're designing a product you can refuse to use materials that aren't recyclable or that are harmful to people or the environment.

For the types of materials it's good to use or avoid, see p. 64.

The 6Rs — like the 3Rs but with better spelling...

A nice little tip for you here: there's a whole exam paper on sustainable design — which means you're going to get tested on this stuff. So if I were you, I'd make sure I knew these two pages back to front.

The 6Rs

REDUCE

1) The environmental impact of a product can be reduced by keeping <u>waste materials</u> to a minimum and by <u>avoiding unnecessary packaging</u>.

2) Using materials <u>economically</u> (e.g. designs that <u>tessellate</u>) will produce <u>less waste</u>.

Squeezing loads of these nets on to one sheet of card will reduce waste material.

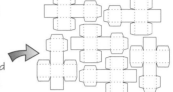

Built-In Obsolescence

1) Some products have what's known as '<u>built-in obsolescence</u>'.

2) This is when a product has been <u>designed</u> to become <u>useless</u> (e.g. paper cups) or <u>out-dated</u> (e.g. a T-shirt with a slogan) quite <u>quickly</u>.

3) Making <u>long-lasting</u>, <u>durable</u> products instead would <u>reduce</u> the number of products customers need to buy. Manufacturers would then make fewer products and so <u>cut down</u> on <u>energy use</u>, <u>transport</u> and <u>materials</u>.

RETHINK

1) You might be able to <u>make</u> the product work in a <u>different way</u>, e.g. a radio that you <u>wind up</u> instead of running off batteries.

2) Or you might be able to make a product that uses much <u>less energy</u> — e.g. <u>energy-efficient</u> light bulbs instead of traditional ones.

3) You could also make a product with many functions — for example, a mobile phone with an alarm clock and a camera is <u>three</u> products in one. This saves on <u>resources</u>, <u>manufacturing processes</u> and <u>disposal</u>.

REPAIR

28 The NORTH
Leeds
Sheffield

Mansfield
A 38

Matlock
(A 615)

1) It's better to maintain and <u>fix</u> things instead of throwing them away and replacing them as soon as they break.

2) This means <u>designing</u> things so they're <u>easy to repair</u> — a simple design with easily accessible parts is best.

3) Products that can be repaired include things like <u>road signs</u>. Their surfaces are designed to be <u>easy to clean</u> and they have a <u>panelled structure</u> — so you can replace individual panels rather than the whole thing.

Practice Questions

1) Name <u>three</u> materials that can be recycled.

2) How is recycling <u>different</u> from reusing?

3) a) What is meant by <u>built-in obsolescence</u>?
   b) Why is built-in obsolescence usually <u>bad</u> for the <u>environment</u>?

4) Bob is designing some disposable plastic cutlery.
   Suggest how he could use the <u>6 Rs</u> to reduce the cutlery's impact on the environment.

Section 5 — Social and Environmental Issues

Sustainable Production

Sustainable Products are Better for the Environment

1) Sustainability means not causing <u>permanent damage</u> to the environment and not using up <u>finite resources</u> (ones that'll <u>run out</u> eventually).

2) How sustainable a product is depends on the <u>design</u> itself — how long-lasting and efficient the product is.

3) It also depends on the <u>materials</u> and <u>processes</u> used to make the product...

Choose Your Materials Carefully

1) Some materials come from <u>renewable resources</u> (ones that can be replaced as fast as we use them). Others come from <u>finite resources</u> (ones that'll run out eventually).

Products and their packaging are often made of <u>plastic</u>. Most plastic is made using <u>crude oil</u> — a <u>finite resource</u>.

Materials like <u>paper</u> and <u>cardboard</u> are more <u>sustainable</u>. They come from <u>trees</u>, which are <u>renewable resources</u> (you can grow more trees to replace those cut down).

2) Some materials are <u>recyclable</u> or <u>biodegradable</u> (they'll break down naturally over time). Others will just end up being chucked in <u>landfill</u>.

Most plastics <u>don't biodegrade</u> — if they're not recycled, they tend to clog up landfill sites.

Paper and card are <u>recyclable</u> and <u>biodegradable</u>.

Processes Have Environmental Impacts Too

1) Some processes use a lot of <u>energy</u>, e.g. <u>moulding plastic</u>. This energy is usually generated from <u>finite resources</u> such as oil, coal and gas.

> The environmental impact of these processes could be <u>reduced</u> if <u>renewable</u> energy sources were used, e.g. <u>wind power</u> or <u>hydroelectricity</u>.

2) Some processes produce a lot of <u>waste</u> or <u>pollution</u>. This can be anything from <u>excess materials</u> to <u>hazardous chemicals</u> like dioxins (see next page), and <u>carbon dioxide</u> — a <u>greenhouse gas</u>.

> It's important to think about how this waste will be <u>disposed</u> of (see p. 66), but also how it can be <u>reduced</u>. For example, using wind power instead of burning coal will cut down on carbon dioxide emissions.

Recycle your material — reuse old jokes...

The <u>nice thing</u> about learning all this stuff is that a) the examiners will be <u>over the moon</u> and give you lots of <u>lovely marks</u>, and b) you'll get to <u>save the planet</u>. Wonderful. Everyone's a winner.

Sustainable Production

Some Chemicals Harm the Environment

The processes used to make many everyday products often use or produce harmful chemicals...

DIOXINS

1) Dioxins are chemicals formed in production methods that use chlorine — this includes the bleaching of wood pulp to make paper and card.

2) Dioxins get into the air, soil and water sources and build up in the food-chain. At high concentrations they can poison both humans and wildlife.

3) The emission of dioxins is now tightly controlled. Some organisations are also encouraging the use of unbleached paper products where possible.

VOCs

1) VOCs (volatile organic compounds) are gases given off by a lot of paints, varnishes and solvents.

2) VOCs are major air pollutants, but they can also get into soil and water. Some are greenhouse gases and many are toxic to humans.

3) Products with fewer VOCs are becoming available, e.g. 'low VOC' or 'VOC-free' paint.

CFCs

1) CFCs are a group of gases that used to be used as a propellant in aerosols.

2) When CFCs get into the upper atmosphere they break down the ozone layer. This is bad news because the ozone layer protects the Earth from the Sun's harmful UV radiation.

3) Using a lot of CFCs was making a 'hole' in the ozone layer and letting through more UV radiation.

4) The use of CFCs has now been reduced — very few aerosols have them in today.

Practice Questions

1) a) What does the term renewable resource mean?
   b) What does the term finite resource mean?

2) Nigel is designing carrier bags for a new shop.
   Explain why it would be better for the environment for him to make the bags out of paper rather than plastic.

3) Suggest how a company that manufactures plastic bottles could reduce the environmental impact of their plastic moulding process.

4) Why are CFCs bad for the environment?

5) Sarah is painting a placard for a 'stop the trees' march. She chooses VOC-free paint to do it with. Why is this better for the environment than if she had chosen ordinary paint?

Use and Disposal

So you've made your product. It looks lovely. The big question is — does your product damage the environment when it's <u>used</u>, and when it's eventually <u>thrown away</u>?

Think About How Your Product Will be Used

1) <u>Using</u> your product could damage the environment. E.g. <u>electrical products</u> use electricity generated by burning <u>fossil fuels</u>, and <u>paint</u> gives off <u>toxic fumes</u>.

2) It's important to keep this in mind when thinking about the <u>environmental impact</u> your product will have. You might be able to change your <u>design</u> to <u>reduce</u> this impact, e.g. by using a <u>solar-powered charger</u> rather than a standard one.

Throwing Away Old Products Causes Pollution

Part of designing and making a product should involve thinking about how to <u>get rid of it</u> — waste disposal can cause <u>big problems</u> for the <u>environment</u>.

1) At the end of its life, an old product needs to be <u>disposed of</u> to make way for a shiny new one. Many products are disposed of in <u>landfill</u> sites. This isn't good for the environment at all — it takes up lots of <u>space</u> and <u>pollutes</u> land and water (e.g. paint can wash off products and into rivers).

2) If waste can't be recycled it needs to be disposed of in a way that's <u>safe</u> for <u>humans</u> and <u>wildlife</u>. One big problem is caused by the <u>plastic shopping bags</u> we use. Many of these end up in the sea where they can kill animals — animals such as seals and turtles mistake them for jellyfish and try to eat them.

3) Designers need to find ways to reduce the amount of material that ends up in landfill sites, e.g. by reducing the amount of <u>packaging</u> they use for products, or by using <u>recyclable materials</u> whenever possible.

Recycling Can Help But Has Some Problems

<u>Recycling</u> products rather than throwing them away can save <u>money</u> and <u>energy</u> — and help protect the <u>environment</u>. Recycling <u>isn't</u> all <u>plain sailing</u> though:

1) Products made from more than one material can be <u>hard to separate</u> into recyclable stuff — clear <u>recycle labelling</u> helps with this (p. 67).

2) It can sometimes be more <u>expensive</u> to recycle old materials than to use new ones.

3) <u>Environmentally unfriendly by-products</u> can be produced in the recycling process, which kinda defeats the point a bit.

4) Recycled material isn't exactly like new material. For example, paper that's been <u>printed</u> on can be recycled, but the ink content means the recycled paper will be <u>darker in colour</u> or have a <u>speckled appearance</u> — and it wouldn't be environmentally friendly to <u>bleach</u> it white again. (There are de-inking processes but these aren't perfect either.)

Glass usually needs to be separated into different colours before it can be recycled.

What a lot of old rubbish...

So, landfill = <u>baaaad</u>, recycling = <u>sort of good</u> — depending on the <u>material</u> and providing that everything's <u>properly labelled</u> with the <u>right symbols</u> (see next page). There. That wraps that up.

Use and Disposal

Symbols Are Used to Show Recyclable Products

1) The <u>Mobius loop</u> symbol means that the product <u>can be recycled</u>, or that it <u>contains</u> some <u>recyclable material</u>...

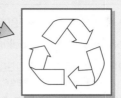

...sometimes the <u>percentage</u> of recycled material is shown.

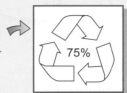

There's also a special Mobius loop for recyclable <u>cardboard</u>.

2) <u>Plastics</u> have their own recycling symbols which help to identify them. They're called <u>SPI symbols</u> and they help recycling plants to <u>sort</u> different types of plastic. For example:

This symbol means it's <u>PVC</u>.

This symbol is found on <u>polystyrene</u> products, e.g. foam cups and protective packaging.

3) The <u>green dot</u> symbol <u>doesn't</u> mean that the packaging is recyclable or will be recycled. It shows that the packaging supplier has contributed to the <u>cost</u> of <u>recycling</u> or <u>recovering</u> the material used.

4) The <u>tidyman</u> symbol means '<u>don't litter</u>' — dispose of the packaging <u>responsibly</u>.

EXAM TIP
Questions pop up in the exam all the time asking you to identify symbols like these — so learn 'em.

Practice Questions

1) In terms of the <u>environment</u>, give <u>two</u> things you should think about when <u>designing packaging</u>.

2) Give <u>two</u> potential <u>problems</u> of recycling material.

3) a) Name this <u>symbol</u>.
   b) What does it <u>mean</u>?

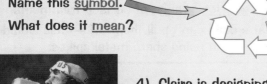

4) Claire is designing a <u>plastic bottle</u> for a sports drink.
   a) What type of <u>recycling symbol</u> could she include on it?
   b) <u>How</u> will this help her bottle to be recycled once it's been used?

Social Issues

There's a lot to think about when you're designing a product...

Products Need to be Accessible for Disabled Users

Lots of products are specifically designed to help people with disabilities. Here are some examples:

1) Packaging often has Braille labelling to give blind people information.
2) Control buttons can be made brightly coloured and extra large, so they're easy to find and press. For example, telephones, TV remotes and calculators can be made with very big buttons.
3) Products such as smoke alarms are designed with visible and audible signs so that deaf and blind people can be alerted to fires.
4) Instructions can be given in picture or diagram form so that people who have difficulty reading text can still use the product.
5) Designers also have to think about wheelchair users. For example, trains and buses need to be designed to have wheelchair access.

Some people will find it easier to use a calculator with bigger buttons.

Designers Need to Think About Age Groups

People in different age groups have different physical limitations. For example:

1) Small children and old people may not be able to manipulate small parts and may have difficulty undoing fastenings, opening packaging or holding and using products.
2) Designers need to think about ways to help these groups of people. For example, they could put large, easy-to-grip handles on products like cutlery.

Sam was having trouble holding the fish — the handle was too small.

Products Must be Safe to Use

1) Think whether people could hurt themselves while using the product.
2) Sometimes it's impossible to avoid potential harm completely (e.g. sharp tools), but for these products you should at least try to minimise the risks.

- Think whether the product could be dangerous if it's misused. You could put instructions and/or safety warning labels on the product to try and stop misuse.
- Make sure your design is ergonomic and won't cause long-term health impacts. For example, a chair with a badly designed backrest could cause awful backache after long-term use.
- Products shouldn't have unnecessary sharp corners or edges for people to cut themselves on.
- Toys often end up in children's mouths, so don't finish the surface with a toxic paint or varnish. Check this out at the research stage and choose a non-toxic range of surface treatments.
- Small components must be firmly attached so that a child can't pull them off — this would be a choking hazard. They must be safely attached too — not using sharp metal spikes.

My social issues have nothing to do with you...

There are a lot of different issues on these two pages and you're bound to get asked questions about some of them. Most of it's just plain ol' common sense though, so use your noggin' and you'll be fine.

Social Issues

Not only do you have a <u>moral responsibility</u> to your consumers, you've got a <u>legal responsibility</u> too...

There Are Laws About Product Safety and Quality

Manufacturers who produce <u>unsafe</u> or <u>unreliable</u> products are probably <u>breaking</u> one of these <u>laws</u>:

1) <u>Consumer Protection From Unfair Trading Regulations</u> ensure that any claims made about a product (e.g. that it is hard-wearing, long-lasting, waterproof) must be true.

2) <u>General Product Safety Regulations</u> state that nobody can put a product on the market unless it's safe.

3) <u>The Sale Of Goods Act</u> ensures that products perform as you would expect and that goods last a reasonable length of time.

4) <u>Fire Safety Regulations</u> cover upholstered furniture and cushions, etc. to ensure that they don't catch fire easily and don't give off really toxic fumes when they burn.

The Vanishing Act

There Are Initiatives for Better Working Conditions

The <u>Ethical Trading Initiative</u> (ETI) was set up to address concerns about products being made by <u>child labour</u> or in factories with <u>poor working conditions</u>.

1) The ETI supports <u>better conditions</u> for workers in <u>developing countries</u>.

2) It's a group of <u>companies</u>, <u>trade unions</u> and <u>volunteer groups</u> from all over the world.

3) Companies in the ETI agree to meet <u>standards</u> covering things like <u>wages</u>, <u>working hours</u> and <u>health and safety</u>.

4) The ETI <u>checks</u> that companies are following the rules and gives members <u>advice</u> about how they can improve.

Practice Questions

1) Explain why some calculators are made with very <u>large buttons</u>.

2) Frank is designing a tin opener.
   a) Suggest how he could make sure it's suitable for <u>elderly people</u>.
   b) <u>Explain</u> your answer.

3) Name a product where it's impossible to completely prevent potential harm. Explain why.

4) Give <u>two ways</u> of making sure toys are <u>safe</u> for children.

5) Katie is designing a bed.
   She is assessing whether her product will break any <u>laws</u>.
   Which laws cover the following things?
   a) Whether the bed will last a long time.
   b) Whether the mattress will give off toxic fumes if it catches fire.

Safety

Employers *have to Provide* Safe Working Conditions

1) The Health and Safety at Work Act (1974) was passed to make sure employers provide a safe working environment, and that they use safety signs to help reduce the risk of accidents.

2) It's the law that employers and workers must use safe working practices at all times.

3) It's also important that workshops have a clear accident procedure (a set of instructions) so that people know what to do if there's an accident and how the accident should be reported.

4) Accidents in industry are kept on file and investigated to make sure they don't happen again.

Safety Advice *Should be Followed*

A lot of this is common sense. But it's incredibly important, so pay attention...

Wear Appropriate Clothing

1) While working (especially with machine tools) make sure your sleeves are rolled back, your tie and apron strings are tucked in and if you've got long hair, it's tied back.

2) Protect yourself from hazardous materials by wearing strong protective gloves and goggles.

Care Should be Taken with Tools and Machinery

1) Always use a safety rule and cutting mat when using knives.

2) Always secure work safely — e.g. clamp work securely before cutting.

3) Know how to switch off and isolate machines in an emergency.

4) Never adjust a machine unless you've switched it off and isolated it.

5) Never leave machines unattended while they're switched on.

6) Don't use machines or hand tools unless you've been shown how.

7) If dust is a danger, e.g. when you're machining board, make sure there's adequate ventilation and that dust extraction equipment is working.

8) Carry tools safely.

Handle Materials and Waste Sensibly

1) Make sure materials are safe to handle — sand down rough or sharp edges on board or plastic.

2) Lots of varnishes and glues (e.g. acrylic cement) give off harmful fumes. So make sure there's good ventilation.

3) Beware of red-hot heating elements (e.g. on hot wire cutters) and naked flames — and keep them away from flammable substances, e.g. aerosol adhesives.

4) Make sure you dispose of waste properly — this is also an environmental issue.

5) When storing material, make sure it's put away safely so it can't fall and injure anyone.

6) Never clear away sawdust with your bare hands — use a brush.

Careful — you'll have someone's eye out with that...

Safety might not be the most thrilling part of graphics, but it is pretty darn important. I'm sure you're fairly attached to your fingers — if you want to keep it that way, make sure you learn these pages.

Safety

Risk Assessments Should be Carried Out

1) A <u>risk assessment</u> is an <u>evaluation</u> carried out by an employer to <u>identify</u> and <u>minimise</u> any potential risks at work. A risk assessment has to be carried out when any <u>new project</u> is being planned.

2) Risk assessments are especially important wherever <u>chemicals</u> or <u>machinery</u> are being used.

3) When you're writing a risk assessment think:

> 1) What could be a <u>hazard</u>?
> 2) What <u>precautions</u> could I take to make sure the risk is minimised?

EXAM TIP
Each hazard and each precaution could be worth one mark. That's <u>a lot</u> of marks altogether.

Hazard	How to reduce the risk
Clothing could get caught in the sanding machine.	Tuck clothes in and wear an apron.

Symbols are used to Tell People About Safety Risks

Blue circles — tell you something you <u>MUST</u> do.

E.g. **EYE PROTECTION MUST BE WORN**
Found on machines which could cause <u>objects to fly</u> towards the user, such as <u>lathes</u> or <u>pillar drills</u>.

Red circles — tell you something you <u>MUST NOT</u> do.

E.g. **NO ENTRY**
Used to stop <u>unauthorised</u> people gaining access to a potentially <u>dangerous</u> area.

Yellow triangles — warn you of a potential HAZARD.

E.g. **HIGH VOLTAGE**
Used to show that there is a risk of electric shock when entering certain areas.

Orange squares — tell you about <u>DANGEROUS CHEMICALS</u>.

E.g. **FLAMMABLE SUBSTANCE**
Found on bottles containing chemicals that <u>easily burn</u> or <u>ignite</u>.

Practice Questions

1) Why is it important to have an <u>accident procedure</u>?

2) What <u>safety precautions</u> should you take if you are:
   a) working with a machine tool?
   b) making a lot of dust while sanding?
   c) working with solvent?

3) Helen needs to carry out a <u>risk assessment</u> for mounting some display work onto board. Make a list of <u>hazards</u> and <u>precautions</u>.

4) What do <u>triangular yellow</u> safety symbols warn you about?

Computer Systems

So, here's a spot of <u>Computer Aided Design</u> and <u>Computer Aided Manufacture</u>, or CAD/CAM to its friends.

CAD *is Designing Using a Computer...*

EXAM TIP
You might have to explain how CAD/CAM could be used to design and make a product.

1) Computer Aided Design (CAD) involves <u>designing products</u> on a <u>computer</u>, rather than using the traditional methods on paper (pages 52-55).

2) CAD packages include <u>2D software</u> (e.g. TechSoft 2D Design) and <u>3D modelling software</u> (e.g. Pro/ENGINEER® and SolidWorks®).

3) CAD helps designers <u>model</u> and <u>change</u> their designs quickly. It's easy to experiment with alternative <u>colours</u> and <u>forms</u> and you can spot problems <u>before making</u> anything.

4) In 3D programs, you can view the product from <u>all angles</u>.

...and *CAM is Making Using a Computer*

1) <u>CAM</u> is the process of <u>manufacturing</u> products with the help of <u>computers</u>.

2) CAD/CAM means linking CAD and CAM together...

3) The CAD software uses <u>numbers</u> to represent each point on your drawing. These are the point's <u>x,y,z coordinates</u> — x is its left/right position, y is forwards/backwards and z is up/down.

4) <u>CAM machines</u> are <u>computer numerically controlled</u> (CNC). Their onboard processor 'reads' the numerical information (the x,y,z coordinates) from the CAD design — and uses these numbers to move its built-in tools to the correct positions to cut out or build up your design.

5) Some <u>milling machines</u> are CAM machines. They <u>remove</u> material from a larger piece of material to shape and create a product.

milling machine

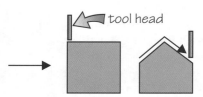

tool head

The machine cuts material away to create the product.

6) Other examples of CAM machines are <u>CNC routers</u>, <u>laser cutters</u> and <u>laser printers</u>.

CAM Increases *the Quality and Quantity of Production*

1) CAM produces <u>high quality</u> products <u>consistently</u>, because machines can be <u>programmed</u> to make exactly the same thing very accurately, <u>over</u> and <u>over</u> again.

2) Humans can't work like this — when lots of products are made by <u>hand</u> there are more <u>mistakes</u>. This <u>reduces quality</u> and <u>wastes</u> time and materials.

3) Also, <u>machines</u> don't need breaks, so they can work <u>longer</u> and <u>faster</u> than humans. So <u>more products</u> can be made in a <u>shorter time</u> (with fewer workers needed).

Learn this CAD/CAM stuff — or you'll look like a right tool...

<u>CAD</u> and <u>CAM</u> are all the rage in product design circles these days. Everybody's at it — not surprising considering how useful they are. Sadly, that means examiners love <u>testing</u> you on it. Those cads...

Computer Systems

CAD/CAM *is Useful for Making Models...*

CAD/CAM can help with the modelling process (see p. 18).
- You can make virtual models (in 3D) using CAD.
- You can use CAD/CAM to do rapid prototyping.

You can design on screen, then use a rapid prototyping machine —
a 3D printer that converts your design into a 3D model.
Stereolithography and laser sintering can also be used for rapid
prototyping but they're much slower and more expensive.

...and for Manufacturing at Different Scales

CAD/CAM can be used to make anything from a single prototype model, right up to the
mass production of thousands of the same item.

One-off production

- In school you might use a 3D printer for modelling, or a laser cutter to produce parts for
  a one-off product.
- In industry, manufacturers also use rapid prototyping (see above) to make prototypes.
  They can show these to the client and check the design before large-scale production starts.

Batch production

- You draw your design once in CAD.
  The CAM machine can then make the batch of products.
- Rapid manufacture means using a rapid prototyping process to manufacture a batch of
  products or components, instead of a traditional process like moulding. At the moment
  rapid manufacture isn't widely used — but this could change as the technology develops.

Mass production

- For example, a CAM lathe could be used to make stair spindles for a furniture company.
- CAD/CAM systems that are suitable for mass production are expensive. But they save
  money in the long run because lots of products can be made very accurately and quickly.

Practice Questions

1) a) Give an example of a piece of 3D CAD software.
   b) Suggest why it might be a good idea to use CAD to design a product.

2) a) What is CAM?
   b) What is meant by CAM being 'computer numerically controlled'?
   c) How does CAM increase the quality of production?

3) Billy wants to make a paperweight from a block of plastic.
   a) Explain how CAD/CAM could be used to do this
   b) Explain how CAD/CAM could help him make a prototype of the paperweight from his designs.

Computer Systems

Information and Communication Technologies — another big mouthful, so let's just call it good old ICT.

Using ICT has its Good and Bad Points

It's not like the old days — ICT is being used more and more in industry. ICT includes everything from computers to robots to computer-controlled machinery. This has both pros and cons:

PROS

1) ICT can increase the amount of work done. This makes businesses more productive, and so more competitive.

2) Workers benefit if ICT can do boring, repetitive tasks leaving them free to do the interesting jobs.

3) Transferring data electronically (see below) is quick and convenient.

4) The Internet is really useful as a research tool — it contains loads of information.

CONS

1) It's expensive to keep investing in the latest and most efficient technology, and it takes time and money to retrain staff.

2) There may be job losses as ICT replaces people for some tasks, e.g. assembling boxes.

3) Continued use of computers can cause health problems, e.g. repetitive strain injury.

ICT is Made Up of Hardware and Software

1) Computer hardware is all the stuff that's, errr... hard and you can move about — like the computer monitor, keyboard, printers and so on.

2) Computer software is the computer programs. You can get ICT software for loads of different things:

- You can use spreadsheet software for working out production costs and time management.
- Painting software is really useful for manipulating photos (see page 46) — you can use software like Paint Shop Pro and Adobe® Photoshop®.
- If you want to create a slideshow to present a design to your client, there's also software for putting together a presentation.

Data can be Stored Electronically

Computers are absolutely great at storing enormous amounts of data (information).

1) Saving work to the hard drive of a computer means you can open it again later on that computer.

2) Computers can be joined together to form a network. Saving your work onto a network means that any computer on that network might have access to it. This could be really useful (you could access your work from other places) or a security nightmare (other people might be able to see your work).

3) Saving it on an external device means that you can carry the data round with you. You can store your work on a memory stick, disc or external hard drive. This can then be plugged into any computer and the files can be opened again.

4) The safest thing to do is save copies of your work in a few different places, e.g. on the computer and on an external device. This is called backing up, and it means that even if you lose one copy of your stuff, it won't be gone forever.

This is dead easy — it's just data-day stuff...

OK, so I'm sure you know the difference between hardware and software, and how to save stuff onto a computer. But what about Electronic Data Interchange and teleconferencing... Oh what joys await you.

Computer Systems

File Format is the Type of File You Save

Different software programs make different types of files *(see page 46 for different types of graphics file)*.

1) The different file types are identified by a code that comes after the file name. It shows you what type of program the file can be opened in.

my_stuff.doc — file name, text document

dog_handstand.jpeg — photo

2) If you make a file using a particular piece of software, and then try and open it on a computer that doesn't have the same software, it won't be able to read the file.

File Size Matters

File size is important when you're saving and sharing data.

1) Some files are much bigger than others. Text files are often pretty small. Images (e.g. drawing or photo files) are usually much bigger.

2) The bigger a file is, the longer it takes to share it, e.g. an e-mail with a picture attachment can take a long time to download.

The Electronic Transfer of Data is Useful for Industry

1) Data can be transferred electronically — from one computer to another. This means that designing and manufacturing can be done in different locations — the designer's work can be electronically transferred to the manufacturing site.

2) E-mail can be used to quickly transfer written information and attachments (e.g. designs) between different locations.

3) Electronic Data Interchange (EDI) is the direct transfer of information from one computer system to another, usually via the telephone network.

4) Teleconferencing allows meetings between workers in different locations. A camera connected to a computer is linked to the telephone network or the Internet. Voices and moving images are relayed in real time.

Practice Questions

1) Suggest two pros of using ICT in industry.

2) a) Give two examples of computer hardware.
   b) What is computer software?

3) Anna needs to save the computer files for her Graphics project.
   a) Suggest three different ways she could do this.
   b) Why is it a good idea for her to back up her work?

4) Anna e-mails Dan a photo he needs for his project. It's taking a long time to download the attachment. Why might this be?

5) A graphic designer has been asked by a client to develop a series of posters and brochures to advertise a new holiday resort. Explain how the electronic transfer of data could be used to help develop the very best product.

Mechanisms

Mechanisms are a great way of making products <u>stand out</u> and <u>appeal</u> to consumers.

Mechanisms can Attract Customers

1) Mechanical systems are used in <u>point-of-sale displays</u> and on <u>packaging</u> to grab people's <u>attention</u> and persuade them to buy a product.
2) They're also used in <u>cards</u> and <u>books</u> to make them more interesting and <u>interactive</u>.
3) There are many different types of <u>mechanism</u>:

V-FOLD MECHANISMS make things <u>lean</u> at <u>different angles</u>:

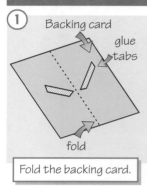

Backing card
glue tabs
fold

Fold the backing card.

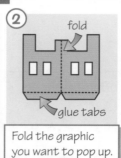

fold
glue tabs

Fold the graphic you want to pop up.

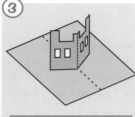

Stick it over the fold on the backing card using the glue tabs.

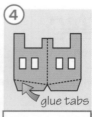

glue tabs

By cutting the glue tabs at an angle...

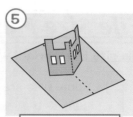

... you can make your graphic lean over backwards.

INTERNAL STEP MECHANISMS make a <u>platform</u>:

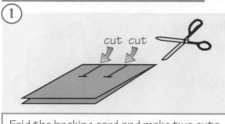
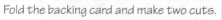

cut cut

Fold the backing card and make two cuts.

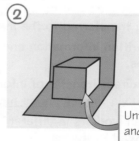

Unfold the backing card and <u>push</u> the step out.

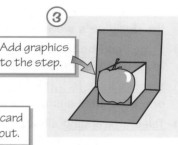

Add graphics to the step.

PARALLELOGRAM MECHANISMS add <u>extra layers</u>:

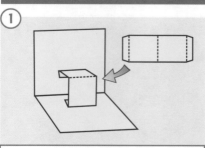

Add the first layer by fixing strips of card to the backing card with tabs.

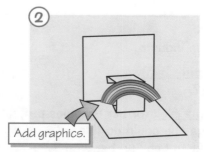

Add graphics.

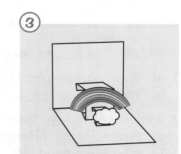

Add more card and graphics to create multiple layers.

It's just cutting and sticking really isn't it...

No, that's not fair — there's a bit of folding too. This stuff also goes by the much fancier name of <u>paper engineering</u>. Oooh. It can be quite <u>fun</u> to do — especially if you start adding <u>slidey bits</u> and <u>levers</u>...

Mechanisms

Levers **Create** Movement

Levers use a <u>pivot</u>. As one end is pushed <u>down</u>, the other end moves <u>up</u>, like a <u>seesaw</u>.

Pulling the string makes the bird's lower beak rotate around the pivot, making it look as if it's closing its beak.

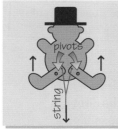

Pulling the string makes the bear's legs rotate around the pivots...

...making it look as if it's kicking its feet in the air.

Levers **Can be** Connected **to Form** Linkages

Levers and linkages move around <u>pivots</u> to change the <u>type</u> or <u>direction</u> of motion.

<u>Split pins</u> are used to <u>link</u> two levers together at a pivot or to let a lever <u>rotate</u>.

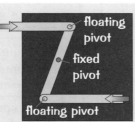

floating pivot
fixed pivot
floating pivot

o <u>Floating pivots</u> join levers together. They aren't attached to the card.

o <u>Fixed pivots</u> are attached to the card and the levers rotate around these points.

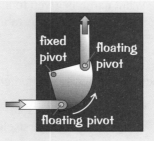

fixed pivot
floating pivot
floating pivot

Discs **Create** Rotary Movement

You can make things <u>spin</u> by attaching <u>discs</u> that move around <u>pivots</u>.

To make the snowman run...

You need to attach a disc like this...

...behind a card with a bit cut out like this.

And the back of the card would look like this...

This is the back of the disc. It's got the feet drawn on the other side.

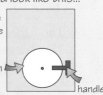

handle

Turning the handle will make the snowman run.

Practice Questions

1) Why might a shop manager decide to use <u>mechanical systems</u> as part of their <u>point-of-sale</u> displays?

2) What is the fancy technical name for:
   a) mechanisms that make graphics <u>pop up</u> at different angles?
   b) mechanisms with <u>platform</u> graphics?
   c) mechanisms with <u>extra layers</u>?

3) Sam wants to make a card with dolphins <u>jumping over</u> some waves. He draws a card with a section cut out, and he makes a disc. Explain where Sam would attach the disc, and what he'd attach it with.

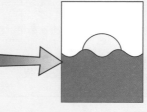

Exam Technique

1) The exam is made up of <u>2 papers</u>. The first is on '<u>Sustainable Design</u>' — it's one hour long.
2) This paper is about all the things you have to consider when designing a product — including all the stages of the <u>design process</u> and the <u>environmental</u> and <u>social</u> considerations.

The <u>Sustainable Design</u> Paper Has <u>Two Parts...</u>

...Section A <u>is</u> Short Answer <u>Questions...</u>

Section A is worth <u>15</u> out of the 60 marks on the paper.

This'll contain <u>multiple choice</u> questions, <u>true or false</u> questions and some questions where you have to <u>write</u> a few words.

1 The abbreviation ETI stands for:

(a) Equality Trading Incorporated
(b) Ethical Training Institute
(c) Environmental Trading Initiative
(d) Ethical Trading Initiative   *(1 mark)*

Read <u>all</u> the answers — don't just go for the first one that sounds possible.

If you <u>don't know</u> the answer to a multiple choice, you might as well <u>guess</u>. You won't lose a mark, and you might get lucky.

2 What name is given to a design which fits the user well in order to be comfortable and limit health problems?

   ergonomic
   (1 mark)

Make sure you've learned all the terms in the <u>glossary</u>.

Decide whether this statement is **true** or **false**.

3 Sometimes products are deliberately designed to become useless quickly.

   True ☑ **False** ☐
   (1 mark)

Don't spend more than <u>a minute</u> on each of these questions — there's only <u>1 mark</u> for each.

...and Section B Contains The Design Question

You'll have to write <u>longer answers</u> in this section. It'll also involve you <u>designing something</u>...

16 The fitness company 'Sports UK' are opening up a chain of sports centres for children. They've asked you to design a logo which will be displayed on the outside of each centre and used in promotional material. The logo must contain the company's name.

a Identify four specification points for your logo.

1. It must appeal to children (e.g. be brightly coloured and eye catching).

2. The logo should reflect the nature of the company (e.g. have a sports theme).

3. It should be able to be reproduced on a range of materials, e.g. on buildings, leaflets, posters, etc.

4. It should be ergonomically designed, e.g. lettering must be large enough to be read from a distance.
   (4 marks)

Think about the <u>target market</u> — the <u>age group</u> is the key thing here.

For some graphic products you could specify <u>production methods</u> and <u>materials</u> so that the product could be manufactured <u>cheaply</u>.

Try to use <u>technical words</u> such as 'ergonomically' — examiners like to see them.

Exam Technique

b Use sketches to show your initial ideas for the logo. Include notes to explain your sketches.

Letters are easy to read, especially from a distance.

Figures of children to appeal to target market.

Brightly coloured to draw the eye.

SPORTS UK

Stylised, modern aerobics figures tie in with fitness theme.

You need to produce a <u>range</u> of ideas — but you don't have time to go overboard. <u>Three</u> is a good number.

To get the full 6 marks you need to use <u>colour</u> and <u>annotate</u> your sketches to explain your ideas. Be as <u>creative</u> as you can.

Tennis player links to sporting theme.

SPORTS UK

Bright red lettering to contrast with the black silhouette.

Make it really, really clear how your design <u>matches</u> each point in your <u>specification</u>. That's what the examiners will be looking for.

Sporting imagery

Bold, capital lettering is easy to read and makes the company name stand out.

SPORTS UK

(6 marks)

Also make sure each design idea is <u>different</u> from the others — you won't get marks if they're too similar.

c Use notes and sketches to develop your best idea.

Football is a popular sport for children.

For the logo outside the sports centre the letters will be cut out using a laser cutter.

Blue outline so the letters leap out at you.

Net, to tie in with football theme.

Will be coloured green to look like grass. This ties in with the football graphic.

Letters are large so that they can be seen from a distance.

(4 marks)

Include as much <u>detail</u> in your notes as possible, even if you think you're <u>stating the obvious</u>.

You need to <u>develop</u> your initial idea. Add some <u>extra features</u> to make it match the specification more closely. Make sure you <u>refer</u> to the points in your specification.

d Explain two ways in which the environmental impact of making and displaying the logo could be reduced.

1. The logo could be displayed on recycled materials, e.g. leaflets made from recycled paper.

2. The logos displayed on the sports centres could be designed to be easily repaired, e.g. have a panelled structure or separate letters so that individual parts can be replaced.

(2 marks)

This whole paper is called '<u>Sustainable Design</u>' — so you can bet your last pair of clean undies that they'll ask you about the sustainability of <u>your</u> design. Bear its <u>eco-footprint</u> in mind right from the start.

Exam Technique

And Now For the 'Technical Aspects' Paper

1) The second paper is on 'Technical Aspects of Designing and Making' — it's 1 hour 15 minutes long.
2) It's also made up of two sections...

...Section A is Just Technical Stuff...

It'll ask you about materials, tools and equipment.

1   The road sign on the right is made from corrugated plastic sheet.

a   Suggest two reasons why this is a suitable material for a road sign.

It's weatherproof so it's suitable for outdoor conditions.

It's rigid so will maintain its shape, staying visible.

(2 marks)

There may be more than two reasons why the material is suitable — but the question is only worth two marks so you only need to put two reasons. You won't get any more marks for writing more and it just wastes time.

b   Item 1 is needed to make the sign. Fill in the details below.

Item 1

Name of equipment metal-cased knife

Use Cutting tough materials, e.g. thick board and plastic sheets.

Safety considerations Use a safety rule to protect your fingers from the blade and a cutting mat to protect surfaces.

(4 marks)

Be specific — say what type of knife it is, or you won't get the marks.

Give as full an answer as possible — give examples of the materials it's used to cut.

Even if you think an answer is too obvious to be what the examiner wants, write it down anyway — some questions will be easier than others. There's no point looking for a more complicated answer.

c *Discuss why a manufacturer might choose to use CAD/CAM to produce large numbers of the sign.

Using CAD/CAM will mean the products are accurate and consistent. The sign can be designed using CAD software and then copied and pasted so that a CAM machine cuts out several at once. The shapes can be arranged on the sheet in the most economical way (to reduce waste) and then cut out at high speed using a laser cutter. The high set-up costs will be recovered by the fast output.

(6 marks)

The asterisk (*) means you can get extra marks for good written communication in this question. So check your spelling and use good English. And think about what you want to say before you start writing so you can put your points in a sensible order.

Exam Technique

...Section B is About Technical Stuff, Design and Sustainability...

Pretty much <u>anything</u> can come up in this section. One of the questions is likely
to ask you to <u>modify</u> a design so it can be used in a slightly different way.

---

4 The drawing below shows the packaging for some
dried fruits called "Froots", made by Yums Snacks.

Question 5: Modify this llama so
that it will also hold 20 DVDs.

a Yums Snacks have decided to change their packaging from
a cylinder to a pentagonal prism. In the space below
draw a net for their new packaging.

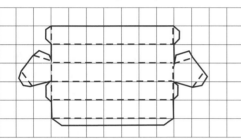

Use a <u>ruler</u> and a <u>sharp</u>
<u>pencil</u> to draw your net.

Remember to draw <u>solid</u> lines to show
which edges to <u>cut</u> and <u>dashed</u> lines
to show which edges to <u>fold</u>. Don't
forget to include <u>tabs</u> in your design.

(4 marks)

b The lettering on the packaging is also changing.
Use the grid below to design a new style of lettering.
It must be the same size as the current style.

Do <u>everything</u> that the question
asks — make sure your lettering is
the <u>same size</u> as the old style.

This is another '<u>Quality of Written</u>
<u>Communication</u>' question — so
check your spelling, grammar and
punctuation and use the proper
<u>technical words</u>.

(4 marks)

c * Yums Snacks aim to make their products as sustainable
as possible. Suggest a material for the packaging and
explain how it contributes to the product's sustainability.

Recycled cardboard would be a good material to use. Card

comes from trees, which are a renewable resource, and using

recycled card would mean no new trees would have been cut

down to make it. This makes it more sustainable than

plastic which is usually made from oil (a finite resource).

The packaging could later be recycled or would biodegrade.

The <u>number of lines</u> you're given
for your answer (as well as the
number of <u>marks</u>) is a big clue to
<u>how much</u> you should write.

When you think you've <u>finished</u>,
go back and <u>read over</u> your
answers to check for <u>mistakes</u>.
You might even think of
something else you could <u>add</u>.

(4 marks)

Glossary

adhesive	Something used to <u>stick things together</u>.
aesthetics	The <u>appearance</u> of an object.
anthropometrics	<u>Body</u> measurement data.
assembly drawing	A drawing showing how the <u>parts</u> of an object <u>fit together</u>.
batch	A set number of identical products that are <u>made together</u>.
binding	Binding is used to <u>hold sheets of paper together</u> in the form of a book.
biodegradable	Something that will <u>decay over time</u>, e.g. paper. (Glass, metal and most plastics are <u>not</u> biodegradable.)
board	<u>Thick paper</u> weighing over 200 grams per square metre (200 gsm).
BSI	British Standards Institution. It <u>sets standards</u> for the <u>quality</u> and <u>safety</u> of products and methods. A product that meets these standards can display the <u>Kitemark</u>.
built-in obsolescence	When something is <u>designed</u> so that it <u>becomes useless</u> or <u>out of date</u> quickly.
CAD/CAM	<u>Designing</u> and <u>manufacturing</u> using a <u>computer</u>.
carbon footprint	The amount of <u>greenhouse gases</u> released by doing or making something.
colour fusion	When tiny dots of <u>different colours</u> really close together <u>blend into a new colour</u>.
contrasting	Contrasting colours are colours that <u>stand out</u> against each other.
copyright	<u>Legal protection</u> which <u>prevents copying</u> of written, drawn or recorded work.
corporate identity	The <u>image</u> that people have of a <u>company</u>, e.g. its personality, style and brand.
corrugated	With a <u>ridged</u> or <u>grooved surface</u>.
crating	Drawing in 3D by starting with a <u>box</u> and taking bits off or adding bits on.
design brief	The <u>instructions</u> that the client gives to the designer about what they want the product to be like.
design specification	A <u>list of conditions</u> that a product should meet.
disassembly	Taking a product <u>apart</u> to see how it's been <u>made</u>.
ecodesign	When the <u>environmental impact</u> of a product is taken into account during its design.
ellipse	A <u>stretched out circle</u>.

Glossary

ergonomic	Easy and comfortable for people to use.
ETI	Ethical Trading Initiative. A group of companies, trade unions and volunteers set up to support better conditions for workers in developing countries.
finite	A finite resource is one that will run out eventually, e.g. crude oil.
fitness for purpose	How well a product does the job that it's designed to do.
fixings	Fixings are used to hold different parts of a product together.
freehand	Drawing without using any equipment — only a pen or pencil.
gap in the market	An area where there aren't any products available to meet people's needs.
gsm	Grams per square metre — the units used to describe different 'weights' of paper or board.
highlight	Lighter colouring used in drawings to show a surface facing the light.
hue	Another word for colour.
ideograms	Pictures that represent objects and ideas — they're often found on signs and packaging.
input device	Something used to enter data into a computer, e.g. a scanner.
laminated	Covered with a layer of another material.
life-cycle analysis	Looking at the environmental impact of a product at each stage of its life.
manufacturing specification	A manufacturing specification tells a manufacturer exactly how to make a product.
market pull	When new products are designed as a result of consumer demand.
market research	Asking the target market what they like or dislike about products, to help you with your design.
mock-up	A full-scale model made of cheap materials used to check the layout of a design.
model	A practice version of a product that you make during the development stage. It's likely to be made from easy-to-work materials and might be scaled down in size.
nanoparticles	Nanoparticles are the really tiny particles involved in nanotechnology.
net	A 2D shape that can be folded to make a 3D object. Also called a surface development.
orthographic projection	A 2D scale drawing of a 3D object showing the front, plan and end views.

Glossary

output device	Something used to transfer data out of the computer, often as a 'hard copy' or product.
perspective drawing	Drawing in 3D so that things that are further away look smaller.
photochromic	Photochromic materials are smart materials that change colour in response to changing light levels.
process colours	The four colours used by colour printers — cyan, magenta, yellow and black.
prototype	A full-size, working, one-off model of a design. A prototype is built to allow evaluation of the product before starting manufacturing in quantity.
quadrilateral	A flat, four-sided shape.
registered design	Legal protection that prevents someone copying a design's shape and appearance.
rendering	Adding shading and/or colour to a drawing to make it look more realistic.
renewable	A renewable resource is one that is replaced by natural processes as fast as it is consumed by humans, e.g. softwood trees in a plantation.
risk assessment	Identifying potential hazards and the precautions needed to minimise risks before work starts.
scale drawing	Scale drawings show objects at different sizes to how they actually are, but still in the right proportions.
sectional drawing	A drawing showing the internal details of an object.
smart material	A material that changes its properties in response to a change in the environment.
sustainable	A sustainable process or material is one that can be used without causing permanent damage to the environment or using up finite resources, e.g. sustainable wood comes from forests where fast-growing trees are chopped down and replaced.
target market	The group of people you want to sell your product to.
technology push	When new products are designed as a result of new technology being available.
thermochromic	Thermochromic materials are smart materials that change colour with heat.
thermoplastics	Plastics that can be melted and re-shaped over and over again.
tone	How light or dark a colour is.
trademark	A word, symbol, logo or slogan that represents a company.
working drawing	A detailed scale drawing that shows all the dimensions of each part of a product, and the materials from which components are to be made, etc.

Answers

Page 5 — New Product Design

1) Market pull is when new or improved products are designed as a result of consumer demand.

2) E.g. drinks cans that tell you when the drink is cool enough.

3) E.g. use card from forests certified by the Forest Stewardship Council / use vegetable-based inks rather than petroleum-based ones.

4) a) E.g. has a nice-looking cover, the layout of the days and weeks is easy to use.
   b) E.g. the printing is clear, the binding is secure.

Page 7 — Design and The Target Group

1) A gap in the market is where there aren't products available to meet people's needs.

2) a) The group of people you're aiming to sell the product to.
   b) People with young children.

3) a) An ergonomic design is easy and comfortable to use.
   b) Any two from, e.g. making the lettering clear and easy to read / what colours will be easy on the eye / making it a suitable size.

4) a) human measurements
   b) E.g. back length, chest width, neck and arm circumference.

5) Most people don't have the average measurements so he's made sure his product will fit the majority of the target group.

Page 9 — Making and Selling Products

1) a) So that customers can recognise their products.
   b) E.g. the name of the company is clear, and it's clear what the company sells.

2) a) Manufacturing, buying and selling on a worldwide scale.
   b) Transport and communication links have improved.
   c) Advantages : two from, e.g. production costs less because it can take place in countries where materials, wages and energy are cheap / savings made in production may be passed on to the consumer as lower prices / customers have a greater product choice / manufacturers can make more money as they have a world-wide customer base.
   Disadvantages: two from, e.g. more energy is used transporting materials and products between countries / more pollution is created transporting materials and products / designing can become complicated as products which need to be sold worldwide have to take a lot of different factors into account / globalisation might reduce the variety of designs worldwide.

3) a) When a product is deliberately designed so that it'll become useless quickly.
   b) E.g. use poor quality materials, e.g. low quality card / make the design really up to the minute, e.g. featuring celebrities.
   c) Advantage — it drives innovation / it keeps designers and manufacturers employed.
   Disadvantage — it's bad for the environment as products are thrown away / making replacement products uses up resources and energy / customers might get annoyed about having to replace the product.

Page 11 — Life-Cycle and Carbon Footprint

1) a) Design that takes into account the environmental impact of the product during its whole life and aims to minimise the negative impacts.
   b) Not causing permanent damage to the environment or using up finite resources.

2) a) A life-cycle analysis looks at each stage in the life of a product and works out the product's potential environmental impact.
   b) Choice of material, manufacture, using the product and product disposal.

3) a) The amount of greenhouse gases released by doing or making something.
   b) Because carbon dioxide is released when they're made, transported and used. This is because fossil fuels are burned to provide the energy for these processes.
   c) E.g. by making a product closer to where it will be sold.

4) By donating money to a project that reduces carbon emissions. The money should help to balance out the greenhouse gases that the company is responsible for.

Page 13 — Product Research

1) a) The job the product is intended to do,
   b) Whether the product does its job well.

2) a) He can take the best bits from other products and incorporate them into his own design.
   b) E.g. a scrapbook
   c) He could find out how the photo album was made.

3) E.g. an upside-down sauce bottle. Sauce bottles with the lid at the top are difficult to get sauce out of. Upside-down bottles are easier to use and make less mess.

4) Make the stand out of cardboard, which does not come from a finite resource and is recyclable. Make the waving clown solar powered rather than battery powered.

Page 15 — Task Analysis

1) a) E.g. what kind of product is needed, how the product will be used, who the product is for.
   b) the client

2) To find out about what people like/dislike about existing products. To see if people will want your product.

3) E.g. conclusion 1: 42% of people preferred the text in blue font. Conclusion 2: 74% of people thought the font size was too small.

4) a) A list of conditions that the product must meet.
   b) E.g. colour / material / production method / size / weight / price range.
   c) E.g. must hold 150 chocolate bars, should have a colourful, shiny surface finish, must have the logo of the chocolate bar, must be no more than 1600 mm tall, must cost less than £4 to manufacture.

Page 17 — Generating Proposals

1) a) E.g. create a mood board / brainstorm some ideas / work from an existing product.
   b) Three sketches, including notes on materials, processes and critical evaluation of ideas, etc.

Answers

2) e.g. a piece of clothing / a piece of furniture

3) E.g. a product with a rude slogan or picture — people may think this isn't appropriate if there are young children around.

4) a) E.g. a Union Jack design.
   b) E.g. he might want to avoid any chance of offending people with strong Christian beliefs.

5) E.g. red might appeal to people with a Chinese background because it's associated with good luck.

Page 19 — Development

1) a) cardboard, balsa wood or expanded polystyrene
   b) E.g. to check the shape of the design / to evaluate it against the design specification / to spot any problems with the design.

2) Prototypes are full-size working products made from the right materials, using the right construction methods. Mock-ups are often made from cheap materials and may not have all the working parts.

3) She could test the prototype scales to make sure they work correctly. If they do, she could ask some people from her target market to use the scales and give her feedback. If the scales work well and people like them she could consider going into larger scale production. If there are problems or potential customers don't like the scales she would try to fix the problems/change the design first.

4) a) Any four from, e.g. Do you like the pop-up features? / What ages do you think they're suitable for? / Do you like the colours? / What don't you like about the cards? / How much would you be willing to pay?
   b) Any four from, e.g. what the cards will be made from / what tools and equipment she will need to make them / how long it will take her to make the cards / how much it will cost to make the cards / how she will put the cards together.

Page 21 — Planning Production

1) a) A manufacturing specification can be a series of written statements, or working drawings and sequence diagrams which explain exactly how to make the product.
   b) Three from, e.g. materials / tolerances / finishing details / costings / quality control checks / sizes

2) Working drawings show the design with the precise dimensions, details of materials, etc., marked on.

3) Put the quality control checks in diamond shaped boxes.

4) a) None of the processes can happen at the same time — each one must happen once the previous one is complete.
   b) 80 minutes
   c) Applying writing and logo — it takes 20 minutes.

Page 23 — Properties of Graphic Materials

1) a) Can absorb impact without snapping.
   b) Light can't travel through it.
   c) Can bend without breaking.

2) a) e.g. an aeroplane window
   b) e.g. a spacecraft

3) E.g. protective packaging needs to resist squashing forces to keep its contents safe.

4) a) e.g. strong, flexible
   b) The material he chooses must be suitable for his chosen production method.
   c) Yes, the frame will be covered with another material and won't be seen, so its aesthetic qualities aren't that important.

Page 25 — Paper, Card and Board

1) Bleed-proof paper — the ink doesn't spread out.

2) a) The surface is textured.
   b) It's used for sketching.

3) They're both translucent / they both let light through.

4) gsm (grams per square metre)

5) Duplex board has only one side smooth for printing. It's used in food packaging because it's unbleached.

6) a) Primary packaging is used for individual items. Secondary packaging is used to hold lots of the same primary-packed items.
   b) Primary packaging — e.g. solid white board.
      Secondary packaging — e.g. corrugated board.

7) E.g. grey board — it's rigid and can be covered with paper for printing.

8) A3

Page 27 — Plastic

1) polyvinyl chloride

2) a) corrugated plastic/corriflute
   b) expanded polystyrene foam/STYROFOAM™

3) a) acetate
   b) PVC

4) A mould is put onto the vacuum bed. A sheet of thermoplastic is heated until it goes soft. The bed is then lifted close to the heated plastic. The air is sucked out from under the plastic. This forces the plastic onto the mould.

5) a) line bending
   b) The element in the line bender heats the plastic along the line where you want to bend it. Once the plastic is soft, it can be bent around a jig.

Page 29 — Smart and Modern Materials

1) A material that reacts to its environment by changing its properties.

2) Quickly constructing/making models to try out new designs.

3) Thermochromic ink — it would change colour when the drink gets too warm, and could be used to reveal text such as 'too warm' or a picture with the same message.

4) They contain a phosphorescent pigment that stores light and slowly releases it. This is what makes them glow in the dark.

5) a) An incredibly tiny particle
   b) E.g. to make anti-vandal paint / to make airtight packaging materials.

Answers

Page 31 — Finishing

1) a) The product will last longer without getting damaged.
   b) Embossing draws attention to a particular bit of the product and can suggest quality.
   c) Foil application also draws attention to a particular bit of the product, e.g. a logo, and can suggest quality.
   d) The product will look smooth, glossy and higher quality.

2) He could laminate them or coat them with varnish.

3) It's a sandwich of thin card with polystyrene foam in the middle. It's used for models and mounting posters.

4) a) aluminium
   b) It will keep flavours in and air out, and seal the sauces inside the carton.
   c) It's hard to recycle because the paper and aluminium need to be separated first.

Page 33 — Joining Materials

1) a) e.g. glue stick / glue pen
   b) an aerosol glue
   c) PVA
   d) superglue

2) Make sure the glue doesn't get on her skin as it's hot.

3) Mix the resin and the hardener together and then apply to the surfaces in a thin layer and stick surfaces together when tacky.

4) E.g. he could use double-sided tape.

Page 35 — Tools and Equipment

1) a) E.g. HB
   b) E.g. 2H

2) E.g. chalk pastels because they're coloured and easily blended.

3) a) A 30-60-90° set square or protractor.
   b) A pair of compasses / compass.
   c) A French curve or Flexicurve.

4) An angle measuring 50°.

5) A circle with a diameter of 6 cm.

Page 37 — Cutting Tools

1) a) a surgical scalpel
   b) a circle cutter
   c) a metal cased knife
   d) scissors / guillotine

2) a) engrave things
   b) packaging, e.g. a milk carton

3) A cutting mat and a safety rule.

4) E.g. an extractor to remove fumes.

Page 39 — Enhancement — Tone and Outlines

1) a) How light or dark it is.
   b) By adding more black or white.

2) A tint is the tone you get by adding white. You get a shade by adding black.

3) Adding shading to a drawing to make it look more realistic.

4)

5)

6) It's time consuming.

Page 41 — Enhancement — Texture

1) highlights

2) a) Any two from, e.g. marker pens / coloured pencils / poster paints.
   b) Use watercolour paints and add a bit of yellow.

3) Put abrasive paper underneath your drawing paper and shade over the top with a coloured pencil / shade using lots of little dots.

4) E.g. use coloured pencils — use more than one colour to get the right shade and use a darker colour to show the grain.

Page 43 — Enhancement — Colour

1) a) Use pale colours.
   b) Any two from, e.g. blue / purple / brown / green.
   c) Red often symbolises danger.

2) a) e.g. black or white
   b) e.g. orange or pink

3) a) primary and secondary colours
   b) primary — red, blue, yellow.
   secondary — orange, purple, green.

4) a) red and blue
   b) yellow and blue

Page 45 — Colour Separation

1) a) cyan, magenta, yellow, black
   b) They add layers of cyan, magenta, yellow and black to create other colours.
   c) To print colours that can't be achieved with CMYK.

2) A colour registration mark. It's used by printers to check the printing plates are aligned in the right position.

3) a) Inkjet and laser printers.
   b) E.g. apart from buying the printer there are no set-up costs.
   c) It's expensive per printed sheet.

4) It gets the drawing into the computer. It does this by separating the image into red, green and blue by taking three pictures at the same time, each using a different colour filter.

Answers

Page 47 — Presentation

1) a) Bitmaps and vector graphics.
   b) bitmaps

2) Two from, e.g. cropping / resizing / rotating / blurring / mirroring / distorting.

3) a) Because the image will probably be copyright.
   b) E.g. photos you've taken yourself / designs you've drawn yourself / images bought from photo image libraries.

4) a) serif
   b) sans serif
   c) serif

5) A traditional serif font would probably be best as the abbey is a historical monument.

6) e.g. a laser cutter

7) a) right-alignment
   b) centre-alignment

Page 49 — Sketching

1) a) When you don't use any drawing equipment apart from a pencil/pen.
   b) Sketching initial design ideas.
   c) To explain details further, e.g. ideas for colours/materials.

2)
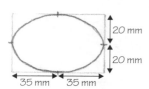

3) a)
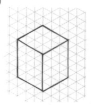
   b) e.g. perspective grid / square grid

4) a) Crating is where you start by drawing a box and gradually add bits on and take bits off till you get the right shape.
   b) e.g.

   c) wireframe drawings

Page 51 — Basic Graphics Shapes

1) right-angled, e.g.   isosceles, e.g.

equilateral, e.g.   scalene, e.g.
          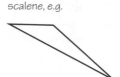

2) equilateral

3) A flat, four-sided shape.

4)

5)
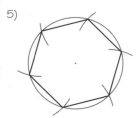

Page 53 — Working Drawings

1) a) The drawing is a quarter of the size of the real fish.
   b) 40 mm. (Height on drawing = 10 mm. 10 mm × 4 = 40 mm.)

2) millimetres / mm

3) a) exploded views
   b) They clearly show how the different parts should be assembled.

4) a) A 3rd angle orthographic projection
   b)
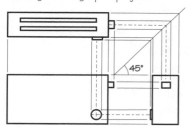

Page 55 — Pictorial Drawings

1) e.g. perspective drawing and isometric drawing

2) A point in the distance on the horizon line where 'parallel' lines appear to meet.

3) a) e.g.   b) e.g.

4) 30°

5) a) isometric drawing
b)

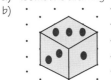

Page 57 — Nets and Packaging

1) They can be used to produce 3D models quickly and cheaply.

2) a) Drawing should show a cuboid structure with an open top, e.g.

b) You cut along these lines.
c) You score and fold along these lines.

3) E.g.

4) E.g.

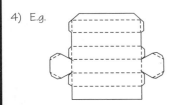

5) E.g. a crash-lock base would provide a secure structure to keep the gerbils the right way up and prevent them from escaping. You could use a slot and tab mechanism for the lid so you could let the gerbils out when you got home.

Page 59 — Charts and Graphs

1) Bar charts use bars to represent information but pictographs use simple pictures/symbols.

2) 100%

3) a) e.g.

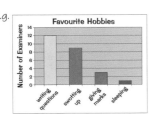

b) e.g.

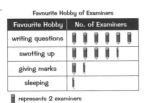

c) e.g.

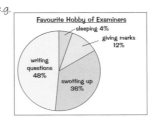

d) E.g. bar chart or pie chart because it's easy to compare the results / pictograph because the information looks interesting.

e) It can't be plotted in a line graph because the data is not continuous.

4) e.g.

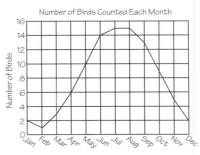

Page 61 — Signs and Labels

1) ideograms / pictograms

2) a) e.g.   b) e.g.

3) This means that the average tin from the batch contains at least 400g of tuna.

4) a) Kitemark
b) The product has met standards set by the British Standards Institution.

5) The product has met EU standards for safety.

6) This means that the product is protected by copyright law so it is illegal to copy it without permission.

Page 63 — The 6Rs

1) Three from, e.g. paper / card / glass / aluminium / steel / some plastics.

2) Recycling involves reprocessing materials so they can be used again. Reusing means using the whole product again.

3) a) Designing products so that they need replacing after a short amount of time.
b) Because more materials and energy have to be used to make replacement products.

4) E.g. recycle — he could use a plastic that is recyclable or recycled, refuse — he could keep packaging to a minimum, rethink — he could design a 'two in one' knife and spoon, etc.

Page 65 — Sustainable Production

1) a) A resource that can be replaced by natural processes as fast as we use it up.
   b) A resource that will eventually run out.

2) Paper comes from trees, a renewable resource, and is biodegradable. Plastic comes from crude oil, a finite resource, and is not biodegradable.

3) By using energy from renewable sources such as wind power for the moulding process rather than energy obtained by burning fossil fuels.

4) CFCs break down the ozone layer. This allows more of the Sun's harmful UV radiation to reach the Earth.

5) VOCs are major air pollutants and greenhouse gases.

Page 67 — Use and Disposal

1) Two from, e.g. how much is needed / how it will be disposed of / if it can be recycled / whether recycled materials can be used.

2) Two from, e.g. it can be difficult to separate materials / it can be expensive / environmentally unfriendly by-products can be produced / recycled materials aren't the same as new materials.

3) a) Mobius loop
   b) That a product can be recycled or contains some recyclable material.

4) a) an SPI symbol
   b) It will allow the type of plastic her bottle is made from to be easily identified at the recycling plant and sorted accordingly.

Page 69 — Social Issues

1) To make them easy to find and press (so that the product is suitable for people with poor vision or limited movement in their hands).

2) a) E.g. it could have a large, easy-to-grip handle.
   b) Older people might have difficulty holding and using a normal tin opener so a larger handle with grips would make it easier for them to use.

3) E.g. a sharp knife — if you made it blunter, it wouldn't do its job.

4) Two from, e.g. make sure they don't have sharp corners / make sure the paint or varnish isn't toxic / make sure components are firmly and safely attached.

5) a) The Sale of Goods Act
   b) Fire Safety Regulations

Page 71 — Safety

1) So that people know what to do if there's an accident and how it should be reported.

2) a) E.g. make sure your sleeves are rolled back and your tie and apron strings are tucked in.
   b) E.g. make sure that any dust extraction equipment is working properly.
   c) E.g. work in a well-ventilated area.

3) E.g.
   Hazard 1) — cutting the display board.
   Precaution — use a safety rule and cutting mat.
   Hazard 2) — using a solvent to stick the work onto the board.
   Precaution — work in a well-ventilated space.

4) Potential hazards.

Page 73 — Computer Systems

1) a) E.g. Pro/ENGINEER® / SolidWorks®
   b) E.g. you can change your design quickly / it's easy to experiment with alternative colours and forms / you can spot any problems before you make your product.

2) a) Computer Aided Manufacture.
   b) The machines follow the x,y,z coordinates from the CAD software, and move the tools to shape the material.
   c) CAM machines are consistently accurate. They make fewer mistakes and so produce less waste than humans.

3) a) He would draw the design using CAD. The software turns this into numerical instructions telling a CAM milling machine how far to move in each direction to shape the plastic.
   b) He could use a rapid prototyping machine to convert his design into a 3D model.

Page 75 — Computer Systems

1) Any two from, e.g. computers can increase the amount of work done / computers can do boring, repetitive tasks, leaving workers to do more interesting jobs / transferring data electronically is quick and convenient / the Internet is a really useful research tool.

2) a) E.g. monitor, keyboard.
   b) The computer programs.

3) a) Three from, e.g. save onto her computer / save onto the school computer network / save onto a memory stick / save onto an external hard drive.
   b) Backing-up means saving work in more than one place. It means that if Anna's work is lost from one place, she will still have other copies of it.

4) The picture might have a very large file size.

5) The designer can work in one location and easily transfer the work to the client in a different location. The designs can be sent as attachments via e-mail, and discussed over the phone. Meetings can be held using teleconferencing. This would help the project move quickly and makes sure the final product turns out exactly how the client wants it to be.

Page 77 — Mechanisms

1) To grab people's attention.

2) a) v-fold mechanisms
   b) internal step mechanisms
   c) parallelogram mechanisms

3) He'd attach the disc behind the card, with a split pin.

Index

Index